in the details. And the electrics are certainly a weak point in these cars. But once these problems are straightened out, your car can be as reliable as any other.

As for the bodywork, corrosion might appear on the 350 GT where the aluminum is wrapped around the steel tubes. This can be expensive to repair and certainly bodywork on an alloy car will be more costly than on one with a steel body. The steel ones, of course, can rust like any other car and this is especially the case with the Isleros. The Bertone-bodied cars will give you fewer problems, as this company took better care of rust proofing its work.

Personally I prefer to buy a car with the original paint work (no matter how bad the paint is) over a car that has just been repainted.

Two people you might need to know: Ing. Giulio Alfieri, general manager of the factory and Jasjit S. Rarewala, president of Lamborghini of North America.

5

In the latter case I am unable to see what has happened to the car and if and how rust problems have been solved. A good bodyman will be able to help you check this point.

If your car needs restoration and you are unable to do the job yourself, try to find a specialist instead of going to your local garage. Not everybody lives near Bob Wallace (the man who did so much for Lamborghini and who knows the cars better than anyone else), who runs a restoration shop in Arizona. But again, a good Ferrari shop will also be able to help you.

If your car is worth the trouble and the money, you can send it back to the factory in Italy. It has a very big department for Lamborghini restoration work, but it refuses to do "half a job" and usually returns a "new" car to the customer.

BRIEF HISTORY

On April 28, 1916, Ferruccio Lamborghini was born, under the constellation of Taurus—thus his love for bulls—in a small farming town near Modena, Italy. As he showed more interest in the mechanical side of farming than the work in the fields, he was sent to a technical school where he graduated just before he was drafted for the army.

He spent the war on the island of Rhodes, first as a soldier, later as a prisoner of war under the British, but always repairing cars, motorbikes and the like. In 1946 he started a little workshop modifying surplus war vehicles into tractors and tuning Fiat 500's and 1100's for sporty drivers. Ferruccio himself drove such a 500 Topolino in the 1948 Mille Miglia and did rather well, until he came off the road after completing only three quarters of the distance.

In 1952 he started building his own tractors, becoming the third largest such company in Italy, behind Fiat and Ferguson. In 1960 he built another factory specializing in oil burners and air-conditioning units. When this new company brought in enough profit he realized his boyhood dream of starting a sports car factory. It became a super modern factory in which he was able to employ the best people from the trade who had been working for companies like Ferrari and Maserati.

Lamborghini never intended to build his cars in large quantities but, like Ferrari and Maserati, produced cars in small series for a few wealthy customers. The factory never made more than 500 cars per year, and that was in the good days, as there were many years when production fell far short of this figure.

They never made many cars of one model either and so far the Espada is the most common with a total of a little over 1,200 units. Compare this with Corvette . . .

In 1969 Lamborghini started another company specializing in hydraulic equipment, which is currently managed by Dr. Tonio Lamborghini, Jr.

In 1972 economics were bad in Italy and Lamborghini sold his tractor factory to a competing company and fifty-one percent of his shares in the car factory to a Swiss businessman named Georges-Henri Rossetti. In the meantime, the Urraco project was costing fortunes in development, the Jarama did not sell as well as expected and worst of all Lamborghini and Rossetti decided to stop the production of the Miura, against Bertone's advice, at the end of 1972.

The new Countach should have followed the Miura and brought the factory into black figures again. This could well have happened— if the car had been ready for sale—but as the situation was, it took years before production really started.

In 1973 the first Urraco came off the production line, but too much was expected of this car. It did sell, but not in the volumes predicted. So when another Swiss businessman, René Leimer, offered to buy Lamborghini's remaining forty-nine percent of the shares, Lamborghini sold them.

The financial situation did not improve, but somehow the factory managed to struggle on. In 1976 a contract was made with BMW to build a sports car (the M-1) for it to race in Group 4, and some were actually built. Unfortunately, a new, money-eating project, the Cheetah, was developed and part of the BMW money disappeared here. BMW canceled the contract and the future looked even worse for Lamborghini.

Walter Wolf, the Canadian Grand Prix team owner and long-time Lamborghini driver, offered to buy the factory, but a deal did not go through. The Swiss owners kept looking for a new buyer and even contacted the Arabs, but did not succeed. The Italian government took over for a two-year period and new people, like Ing. Giulio Alfieri of Maserati fame, were persuaded to come to Sant'Agata.

In September 1979 a German consortium came into the picture and bought the factory for an unknown amount of money. This relationship almost killed the Lamborghini factory, as the Germans hollowed-out the company until the Bologna bankruptcy court found the Germans unsuitable.

In the second half of 1980 the Anglo-French-Swiss Mimran Group leased the factory from the government and now, under the guidance of young Patrick Mimran and with the help of Giulio Alfieri, the factory is slowly rising out of the red figures.

On May 23, 1981, the Swiss Mimran family bought the Lamborghini automobile factory for a price of 3,850,000,000 Lire. The Jalpa 3500, the successor to the Silhouette, was developed and bodies built by Bertone to the drawings of Marcello Gandini. The Countach remained in production, and work was carried out on the LM 001, a newer version of the Cheetah. If someone asked what LM stood for the answer was that it depended on the buyer. It could be Lamborghini-Military or Lamborghini-Mimran.

In 1982, the Countach LP 5000 S was introduced and one year later, in 1983, the first Jalpa was delivered to a customer. In 1979, only forty-three cars were built by Lamborghini but the new masters succeeded in bringing this capacity to 125 Countach and 110 Jalpa in 1984.

Nuova Automobili F. Lamborghini S.p.A. changed hands again on April 23, 1987, and this time Chrysler Motors was the buyer. At that time the annual production was 220 Countachs, seventy Jalpas 160 LM 002s and some 100 engines for off-shore power boats. With Chrysler's money new people, such as Mauro Forghieri and Daniele Audetto were "bought" from Ferrari and new plans, such as a Formula 1 engine, carried out.

Jalpa production was halted on July 27, 1988, and some months later a design exercise of its successor, the P 140, was shown to a select few Lamborghini dealers. At the end of 1991, the final shape was still in doubt but the new car is certain to be a two seater with targa roof and probably powered by a 3.9 liter V-10 engine designed by Ing. Marmiroli, Lamborghini's latest technical director. This small car is planned for market release in 1993. For 1992, a four-wheel-drive Diablo will be added to the program.

In May 1991, there were rumors that Chrysler, who was not doing well in the United States, was trying to sell the Italian company. Names like BMW, Porsche, Peugeot and even Volkswagen were mentioned as prospective buyers. Lamborghini denied all, saying, "Everything is fine here. We are doing well. We can sell more than we can produce and one day our F-1 engine will prove what it promised."

INVESTMENT RATINGS

★★★★★ The best of the Lamborghinis. These cars might be expensive already, but you can be sure that their values will go up.

★★★★ Almost the best. If you can buy one for a reasonable price you can be sure to get your money back plus a good amount of interest.

★★★ These cars too will appreciate in value, though it might take a bit longer. You can be sure that you will not lose money on one.

★★ Still Lamborghinis and as reliable and fast as the more desirable models. These models were almost the same price when new as the real classics; therefore, there is no reason to refuse such a model.

★ No Lamborghini will deserve only one star unless it is a wreck or a car with the wrong engine. Even then it will be worth buying if you have the patience to go shopping for the missing parts. As a "parts-car" it will always be worth money because the spares will fit the more valuable models.

The only real Miura Spider was rebuilt in zinc for ILZRO in 1969 as a show car.

CHAPTER 1
350 GTV

★★★★★

May 15, 1963, was an important date for the Lamborghini factory because on that day the company's new twelve-cylinder engine ran, for the first time, under its own power on a Schenk dynamometer. Giuliano Pizzi, the man in charge, measured 36 mkg at 4500 rpm (226 hp). At 8000 rpm the power was 360 hp, more than Lamborghini had expected and wanted; so the engine was detuned to 280 hp at 6500 rpm.

Giotto Bizzarrini, who had designed the engine from scratch, left Lamborghini at that point to return to his own design studios.

Only one prototype of the 350 GTV was built and the car was introduced to the public at the 1963 Turin motor show. It is still at the factory and when time permits, it will be restored.

Ferruccio Lamborghini explaining his 350 GTV to the not-too-enthusiastic press.

The third seat in the 350 GTV only *looks* like a seat.

The chassis of the 350 GTV was built by the small Modena firm,
Neri & Bonacini.

The 350 GTV photographed in 1963.

Details of the independent rear suspension of the 350 GTV.

The front suspension of the 350 GTV.

The GTV as it was photographed at the factory in 1982.

CHAPTER 2
350 GT

★★★★

When the 350 GTV was introduced, the world was not too excited by the body design. Still, Sig. Lamborghini thought the car promising enough to carry on and start production. The well-known coachbuilder Touring of Milano facelifted the design and built the 350 GT (as the production model was called), in its patented, "superleggera" (super light) way. This was done by fixing the very thin aluminum plating to a frame of steel tubes, thus saving weight. The pop-up headlights were replaced by two twin headlight units, but the basic lines of the original car were kept.

Mechanically, the differences were to be found in the engine. The 350 GT had six horizontal Weber carburetors, instead of the GTV's vertical units; a wet-sump lubrication; and two Marelli distributors, which were moved to the front of the engine for easier servicing.

The car still had independent suspension on all four wheels and servo-assisted Girling disc brakes, the front discs with a diameter of 30 cm (11.7 in.), the ones on the rear wheels being 28 cm (10.9 in.). It came with a fully synchronized five-speed gearbox made by ZF in Germany, a firm also responsible for the steering box of the worm and screw type.

The 350 GT was introduced at the Geneva motor show held in March 1964. That year, thirteen cars, starting with chassis number 0102, were built and sold.

In 1965 the 350 GT could also be had with a four-liter engine (bore was 86 mm, instead of 77 mm) which gave the car 50 more horsepower. For the 1965 New York motor show the factory built a special 350 GT with a four-liter engine and six vertical Weber carburetors, but this model never went into production.

Other specials that were introduced in 1965 were a coupe built by Zagato and a convertible by Touring. Of the Zagato car, two were built. Of the Touring convertible, two or three were made.

The 350 GT was more sophisticated than the Ferraris of those days. It lacked the "sporty" exhaust noises, but was technically far more interesting and advanced. The Lamborghini had four overhead camshafts instead of two, carried six carburetors instead of three, had independent suspension on all four wheels and a five-speed gearbox instead of a four-speed box with a clumsy overdrive as on the Ferrari 330 GT. Power-operated door windows were standard and the body was made in aluminum instead of steel. The body line was perhaps not to everyone's taste, but certainly more modern than Ferrari's.

The American magazine *Car and Driver* tested the car in March 1966 and wrote: "It is much less demanding to drive than a Ferrari, and,

One of the very first 350 GT's. Note the front bumper in one piece and the different grille.

what is more, it seems to steer, stop, go and corner just about as well as our Ferrari test car (275 GTS), but it is so smooth, and so quiet."

And *Sports Car Graphic* wrote that same month about the riding qualities of the 350 GT: "It excels on every type of surface, from washboard to wavy freeway, transmitting an absolute minimum of jounce or vibration to the passenger. This feature, combined with the roadability, the lack of noise, the engine idle, etc., make it the most enjoyable 150-mph-plus car we've ever ventured into traffic and city driving with . . . . by a big margin."

The 350 GT is a real collector car now, with the only disadvantage being that parts are hard to find.

Model . . . . **350 GT**
Introduced . . . . 1964 Geneva motor show
Number built . . . . 143 including 23 with 4-liter
                 engine (chassis no. 0102-0574)
Production years 1964-66
Engine . . . . V-12 60°
Bore x stroke in mm . . . . 77 x 62 and 82 x 62
Displacement in cc . . . . 3464 and 3929
Valve operation . . . . Double overhead camshafts
                 on each bank of cylinders
Compression ratio 9.5:1
Carburetion . . . . 6 twin-throat Webers, 40 DCOE 2
Bhp . . . . 270 at 7000 rpm and 320 at 6500 rpm
Chassis & Drivetrain
Clutch . . . . . . Single dry-plate, hydraulically operated
Transmission . . . . Five-speed, all-synchromesh
Rear suspension . . . . . . Independent, coil springs and
                 telescopic shock absorbers
Axle ratio . . . . 13/49; on request 11/45, 11/47
Front suspension . . . . . Independent, coil springs and
                 telescopic shock absorbers
Frame . . . . Tubular
General
Wheelbase mm/in. 2550/99.5
Track, front mm/in. 1380/53.8
     rear mm/in. 1380/53.8
Brakes . . . . Girling discs, vacuum assisted
Tire size, front and rear . . . . 205-15 HS Pirelli
                 Cinturato
Wheels . . . . Borrani wire wheels
Body builder . . . . Touring of Milano
Fuel tank capacity . . . . 80 lit/21 gal
Engine oil capacity . . . . 10 lit/10.5 qt
Cooling system capacity . . . . 15 lit/15.8 qt
Overall length mm/in. 4500/175.5
Overall width mm/in. 1730/67.5
Overall height mm/in. 1220/47.5
Dry weight kg/lb. 1050/2310
Top speed kmph/mph 240/148.8

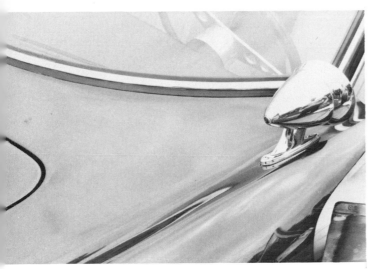

An early car; later cars had two air-intake cowls in front of the windshield.

The inside luggage compartment of the 350 GT, or do you want to call it a rear seat?

One of the very first cars, photographed in the parking lot of the factory.

The very clean 350 GT engine. By using horizontal Webers the body line could be kept low.

Sometime during its production period, the 350 GT received a back-up light mounted underneath the number plate.

350 GT chassis number 0196 is now with Michael Kollins in the US. The chrome ring around the fuel filler cap indicates that this is an early car.

The instrument panel of car 0196. The air conditioning on the left of the dashboard was not standard equipment.

Zagato built only two cars on Lamborghini chassis (number 0310 and 0322); one was shown at the London motor show in 1965. The car had left-hand drive, but was modified to right-hand drive when it was sold to a buyer in Australia. The car had the more powerful 3.5-liter engine.

Only two 350 GTS Spyders have been built by Carrozzeria Touring, chassis numbers 0325 and 0328. The latter was shown at the 1965 Turin motor show and is now in the US. Car number 0325 went to Spain but now belongs to Prince Altani from Saudi Arabia.

On the early 350 GT's, part of the instrument panel was made of polished aluminum. Later versions, like this number 0358, had it leather-covered. Note also the different steering wheel.

The 1966 350 GT number 0358 belonging to the head of the Canadian Lamborghini Club, Ken Browning.

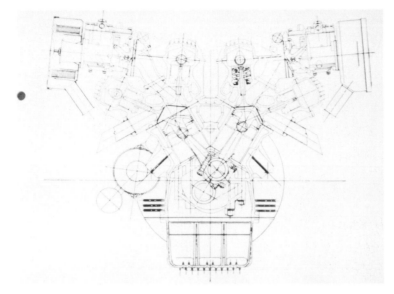

A drawing of the 350 GT engine.

One of the 350 GT's, chassis number 0436, that was sold in Switzerland. Now the car is in the US. The twin headlights had to be replaced to meet American laws.

The interior of the 400 GT was the same as on the 350 GT, except for the steering wheel.

In 1965 the 350 GT could be had with a four-liter engine, which became the basis for the later engines used by Lamborghini. Here is such a 400 GT, as the car was also called (not to be mixed up with 400 GT 2+2), with chassis number 0220, owned by Jim Kaminsky.

Photographed in the professional restoration department of the Lamborghini factory in May 1982. This is a Spyder with chassis number 0160, a number known to me as belonging to a 350 Coupe in France. Are we building replicas already?

CHAPTER 3
400 GT 2+2

★★★

Most of Lamborghini's new models were presented at the Geneva motor show, including the 400 GT which came out in March 1966. The car had the same lines as the two-seater 350 GT, but featured two occasional seats in the rear. The rear window was smaller than that of the 350 GT, but the trunk was larger as only one fuel tank was fitted instead of two small ones. The 350's rectangular headlamps were replaced by four round units on the 400.

Though Touring made the bodies, they were now of steel instead of aluminum. This made the car, which was a bit longer and higher than the 350 GT, 190 kg (418 lb.) heavier. The top speed was about the same as that of the 350 GT with a 3.5-liter engine, 240 km/h (149 mph).

Geoffrey Howard wrote in the April 20, 1967, edition of *Autocar:* "The Vee-12 4-litre engine seems to have the greatest range of smooth torque of any unit we have driven. From as low as 1000 rpm it will zoom sweetly to 7,000 rpm, pulling hard all the way with no perceptible steps in the torque delivery. This, in conjuction with high gear ratios (60 mph in first, 80 mph in second, 105 in third), gives the car the longest legs of any we know. At the end of a quarter mile from rest the speedometer is reading 100 mph with two more gears still to go."

The four-liter engine was the same as used in some of the 350 GT cars, but the ZF gearbox and the Salisbury rear axle were replaced by Lamborghini-built components. Building these parts in its own factory made Lamborghini independent from outside manufacturers and proved that the factory was capable of making the items itself. Actually, the Lamborghini gearbox, using the Porsche synchronizing system, was better and quieter than the ZF units.

A few one-offs were built using the 400 GT 2+2 as a basis. Carrozzeria Touring brought its Spider project to the 1966 Geneva show and presented the Flying Star II, a 2+2 coupe at the Turin motor show the same year. They remained one-offs like the car that Neri & Bonacini made for an American customer in 1966, which was called the Monza 400.

The chances of finding one of the "specials" are small, but finding a good 400 GT 2+2 is still not too difficult as no less than 247 were built between 1966 and 1968, the year Touring went out of business.

For the real car collector this model might not be so interesting as the "first" Lamborghini, the 350 GT, but the car still has some advantages. Finding parts is less difficult, as many mechanical parts were also used in later Lamborghini models. Besides that, a steel body is cheaper to restore than an aluminum one.

The rear window of the 400 2+2 was much smaller than that of the two-seater Lamborghini. The leather-covered instrument panel was very much the same.

The 3929 cc V-12 engine was the same as used in the four-liter version of the 350 GT and was the base for later Lamborghini models.

The 400 GT 2+2 looked very much like its predecessor.

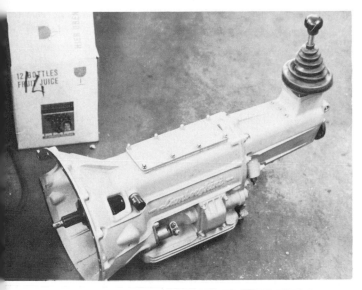

To be independent from outside suppliers, Lamborghini decided to build its own gearboxes and differentials for the 400 series. The gearboxes were of a better quality than those made for the 350 GT by ZF, and the differentials gave fewer problems than those made by Salisbury.

The rear seats of the 400 GT 2+2 look comfortable enough, but do not try to sit on them for very long. . . .

Model	400 GT 2 + 2
Introduced	1966 Geneva motor show
Number built	247 (no. 0403 - 01354)
Production years	1966-68
Engine	V-12 60°
Bore x stroke in mm	82 x 62
Displacement in cc	3929
Valve operation	Double overhead camshafts on each bank of cylinders
Compression ratio	9.5:1
Carburetion	6 twin-throat Webers, 40 DCOE
Bhp	320 at 6500 rpm

Chassis & Drivetrain

Clutch	Single dry-plate, hydraulically operated
Transmission	Five-speed, all-synchromesh
Rear suspension	Independent, coil springs and telescopic shock absorbers
Axle ratio	11/45
Front suspension	Independent, coil springs and telescopic shock absorbers
Frame	Tubular

General

Wheelbase mm/in.	2550/99.5
Track, front mm/in.	1380/53.8
rear mm/in.	1380/53.8
Brakes	Girling discs
Tire size, front and rear	210-15 VR Pirelli Cinturato
Wheels	Borrani wire wheels
Body builder	Touring of Milano
Fuel tank capacity	80 lit/21 gal
Engine oil capacity	10 lit/10.5 qt
Cooling system capacity	15 lit/15.8 qt
Overall length mm/in.	4640/181.
Overall width mm/in.	1725/67.3
Overall height mm/in.	1285/50.1
Dry weight kg/lb	1380/3036
Top speed kmph/mph	250/155

The 400 GT 2+2 had four round Hella headlights, so that sealed-beam units could be fitted. Note, however, that some 350 GT's were modified with these lamps, for the above reason and to make the car look more "modern." Shown here is a 1967 model, with chassis number 0967.

The Italian coachbuilder Neri & Bonacini built this special for an American customer in 1966. The mechanics of the 400 GT 2+2 were used. On April 8, 1967, the car was sold to someone in Spain and is still with the first owner.

34

Another Lamborghini special, the 400 GT Flying Star II—one of the last cars built by Touring before it went out of business. It was shown at the 1966 Turin motor show. The car is now in France.

CHAPTER 4
MIURA

★★★ P 400
★★★★ P 400 S
★★★★★ P 400 SV

Ferruccio Lamborghini had always claimed that he was not interested in car racing and would never build a car for such a purpose. But when he showed a special chassis at the 1965 Turin motor show, people were convinced he had changed his mind. The chassis shown was anything but just another sports car.

This chassis had been built by Giampaolo Dallara, Bob Wallace and Paolo Stanzani in their spare time, without Lamborghini knowing it. They hoped the design would make Lamborghini start building racing cars. It was shown to him in November 1964 and he was enthusiastic about it. It would be a wonderful one-off, a real show car for which Bertone just had to design a body.

Young Bertone stylist Marcello Gandini was honored with the job and produced one of the most fantastic sports cars built so far. Not only at the 1966 Geneva motor show was it an eye catcher, it still is and will always remain so.

The first Miura, chassis number 0509, had been thoroughly tested by Bob Wallace before it was destroyed. Three more prototypes were built before Bertone, with Bob Wallace taking care of the technical problems, found a solution to lessen the heat and noise in the car. Though plenty of orders for the P 400 Miura were at hand, it took Lamborghini and Bertone several months before they had the required parts available to start production. In March 1967 the first car, chassis number 0979, was sent to a customer. That first year no less than 108 Miuras were delivered; in 1968, 184.

The Miura was named after the most famous Spanish breeder of fighting bulls, Don Eduardo Miura.

Miura S

On January 29, 1969, the first Miura S, chassis number 3919, came off the line. The S-version was a better car, having solved many of the early problems the Miura suffered. Air conditioning and electrically operated windows could be had as options and most Miura S cars left the factory on the new Pirelli P 70 radial tires. The interior was modified and showed a lockable glovebox. In the engine, different camshafts and combustion chambers provided more horsepower.

The British magazine *Autocar* tested a Miura S in August 1970 and its summary was: "Fastest car yet tested. Bottom-end acceleration slightly less impressive. Well balanced handling, stable at speed. Ride reasonable, brakes effective. Cockpit rather cramped and luggage room limited. Very noisy exhaust and interior poorly insulated. Satisfying

An American-version Miura, chassis number 3715, with the speedometer running to 200 mph instead of the more impressive-looking 320 km/h.

machine, strictly for millionaires." In their test ride the *Autocar* people achieved a top speed of 172 mph, and reached 140 mph within thirty seconds.

Just 140 Miura S cars had been built when, at the 1971 Geneva motor show, the most perfect Miura, the SV, was introduced.

Miura SV

The Miura SV can be said to have been free of problems. The body received some facelifts, such as wider rear fenders to make room for wider tires. The nose of the car had a bigger grille and bigger parking lights. The eyebrows around the headlights had been removed and new taillights included back-up lights.

Mechanically the car had undergone some changes, too. Different cam timing, bigger inlet valves and modified carburetors gave the engine more power. Reinforced front and rear ends of the chassis gave the car more rigidity. Extensive modifications on the rear wheel suspension improved the handling of the SV.

The first SV had chassis number 4834 and was shown at the 1971 Geneva show. At that same show Bertone displayed the prototype of his Countach, which would become the successor of the Miura, and of course this car got all the attention of the public. As we will see, production of the Countach was delayed by many years. Still, only 120 SV's were built and sold, the last one leaving the factory in 1972 with chassis number 5113. In March 1975, Canadian enthusiast Walter Wolf had a Miura built for his wife from spares. This car had chassis number 5092, but was more a one-off than a production car.

Another famous one-off was Bertone's Miura Spider presented to the public at the 1968 Brussels motor show. In 1969 the car was rebuilt in zinc for the American ILZRO company for demonstrating its materials and renamed the Zn 75.

All over the world Miuras are being converted to roadsters, so it is important to know that only one "real" Spider was made. Also, many P 400 Miuras were modified over the years into S and SV versions; and, therefore, in case of doubt, a buyer should check the chassis number with the factory, which is very helpful.

When this chassis was shown at the 1965 Turin show everybody
was sure Lamborghini was planning a racing car.

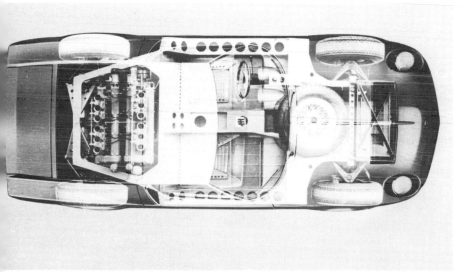

On the first Miuras the heat not only came through the windshield,
but also from the engine.

Model	P 400 Miura
Introduced	1966 Geneva motor show
Number built	475 (no. 0502-4070)
Production years	1966-69
Engine	V-12 60°
Bore x stroke in mm	82 x 62
Displacement in cc	3929
Valve operation	Double overhead camshafts on each bank of cylinders
Compression ratio	9.5:1
Carburetion	1966, 4 Webers 40 IDA 30; 1967, 2 Webers 40 IDA 3C and 2 Webers 40 IDAC; 1968, 4 Webers 40 IDA 30
Bhp	350 at 7000 rpm

Chassis & Drivetrain

Clutch	Single dry-plate, hydraulically operated
Transmission	Five-speed, all-synchromesh
Rear suspension	Independent, coil springs and telescopic shock absorbers
Axle ratio	11/45
Front suspension	Independent, coil springs and telescopic shock absorbers
Frame	Welded box sections

General

Wheelbase mm/in.	2500/97.5
Track, front mm/in.	1400/54.6
rear mm/in.	1400/54.6
Brakes	Girling discs
Tire size, front and rear	205-15
Wheels	Campagnolo cast magnesium
Body builder	Bertone
Fuel tank capacity	80 lit/21 gal
Engine oil capacity	14 lit/14.7 qt
Cooling system capacity	14 lit/14.7 qt
Overall length mm/in.	4370/170.4
Overall width mm/in.	1760/68.6
Overall height mm/in.	1050/41
Dry weight kg/lb.	945/2079
Top speed kmph/mph	280/173.6

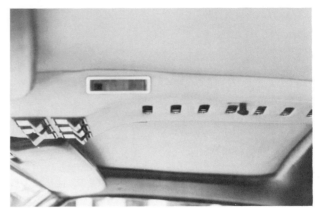

Switches in the roof and fresh-air slots.

Only a very few Miuras were entered in races. Here Gerhard Mitter in the Steinwinter Racing Team car during the Preis der Nationen race at the Hockenheim Ring in 1968. The car did not finish the race.

Mike Nowicki owns this P 400 Miura, chassis number 0979, the first production Miura that was sold by the factory in March 1967.

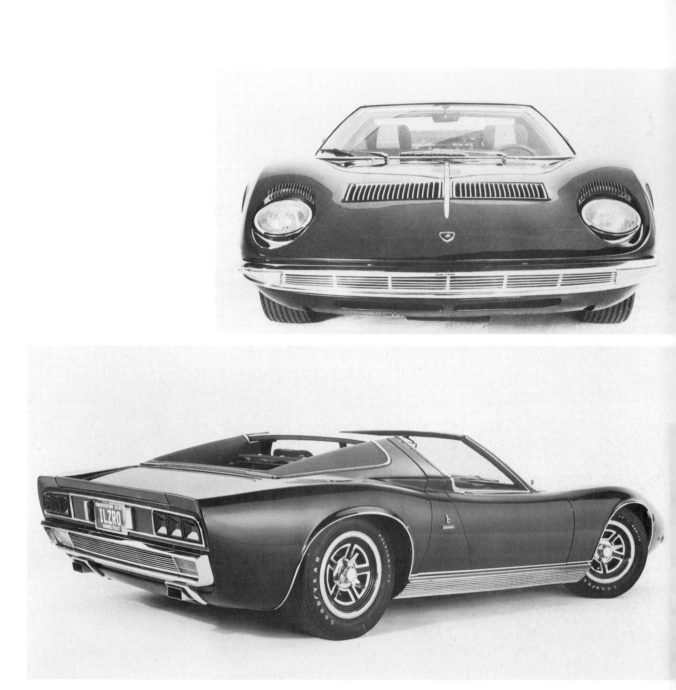

The only real Miura Spider was rebuilt in zinc for ILZRO (International Lead-Zinc Research Organization) in 1969. Zinc was used where possible: carburetor velocity stacks, inlet manifolds, exhaust system, radiator, oil sump, water pump housing, all water lines, bumpers, grille, steering wheel, switches, door handles, shift lever, hand brake, taillights and so on. Lead insulation was used under the floor and in the doors.

A Miura S, chassis number 4149. Good access to the mechanical parts of the car is obvious.

The interior of the S. Note the different steering wheel and the switches for the electrically operated windows. Also new on the S-versions were chromed window frames and headlight rings.

The Miura S, of which 140 cars were built.

The Miura S engine in the foyer of the Lamborghini factory.

Note the ventilated brake discs which were first used on the S-models.

Weight was saved where possible and made the Miura chassis look like Swiss cheese. Here a 1969 S model.

Model	P 400 Miura S
Introduced	1970 Geneva motor show
Number built	140 (no. 4076-4856)
Production years	1969-71
Engine	V-12 60°
Bore x stroke in mm	82 x 62
Displacement in cc	3929
Valve operation	Double overhead camshafts on each bank of cylinders
Compression ratio	10.4:1
Carburetion	4 Weber 3 throat, 40 IDL 3 C
Bhp	370 at 7700 rpm

Chassis & Drivetrain

Clutch	Single dry-plate, hydraulically operated
Transmission	Five-speed, all-synchromesh
Rear suspension	Independent, coil springs and telescopic shock absorbers
Axle ratio	11/45
Front suspension	Independent, coil springs and telescopic shock absorbers
Frame	Welded box sections

General

Wheelbase mm/in.	2504/97.7
Track, front mm/in.	1512/59
rear mm/in.	1512/59
Brakes	Girling ventilated discs
Tire size, front and rear	205-15
Wheels	Campagnolo cast magnesium
Body builder	Bertone
Fuel tank capacity	80 lit/21 gal
Engine oil capacity	14 lit/14.7 qt
Cooling system capacity	14 lit/14.7 qt
Overall length mm/in.	4390/171.2
Overall width mm/in.	1780/69.4
Overall height mm/in.	1100/42.9
Dry weight kg/lb.	1180/2596
Top speed kmph/mph	285/176.7

A partly dismantled Miura S of 1969. The body sections could be removed in minutes, giving access to the major parts. The rear A-arms had been modified on the S-version, and their mounting points repositioned to lessen the squat effect under acceleration.

Luggage space was very limited in Miuras, here a 1969 S-version.

A sales invoice from 1970. The German customer bought his Miura S complete with accessories and hexagon wheel nuts for a price of 6,654,125 —lira, (approximately $21,000). The color of the car was Italian racing red, but the interior was blue.

In 1968 the 205 x 15 Pirelli tires were replaced by the modern GR 70 VR 15 low-profile tires.

The leather-covered interior of the Miura SV.

This Miura SV, number 4806, was delivered by the factory June 12, 1971. The car had several options fitted by the factory, such as a 110-liter fuel tank. It won the Concours d'Elégance in Bad Bürkheim, Germany, in 1981, for its owner, Armin Johl.

A genuine Miura SV, number 5060. Usually the wheels were polished or painted silver, but white looks very good, too. Note the wide grille and the lack of eyebrows around the headlights.

The actual last car of the series was this, number 5110, which left the factory January 15, 1973. The car was built for the Italian industrialist Innocenti, but is now in Switzerland, still in its original black color.

Interesting details of the Miura SV 5110 are the fuel filler cap and the open air box.

Model	P 400 Miura SV
Introduced	1971 Geneva motor show
Number built	150 (no. 4834-5113)
Production years	1971-72
Engine	V-12 60°
Bore x stroke in mm	82 x 62
Displacement in cc	3929
Valve operation	Double overhead camshafts on each bank of cylinders
Compression ratio	10.7:1
Carburetion	4 Weber 3 throat, 40 IDL 3 L
Bhp	385 at 7850 rpm
Chassis & Drivetrain	
Clutch	Single dry-plate, hydraulically operated
Transmission	Five-speed, all-synchromesh
Rear suspension	Independent, coil springs and telescopic shock absorbers
Axle ratio	11/45
Front suspension	Independent, coil springs and telescopic shock absorbers
Frame	Welded box sections
General	
Wheelbase mm/in.	2505/97.7
Track, front mm/in.	1410/55
rear mm/in.	1540/60
Brakes	Girling ventilated discs
Tire size, front and rear	FR 70 VR 15
Wheels	Campagnolo cast magnesium
Body builder	Bertone
Fuel tank capacity	80 lit/21 gal
Engine oil capacity	14 lit/14.7 qt
Cooling system capacity	14 lit/14.7 qt
Overall length mm/in.	4390/171.2
Overall width mm/in.	1780/69.4
Overall height mm/in.	1100/42.9
Dry weight kg/lb.	1245/2739
Top speed kmph/mph	290/179.8

The interior is in white leather, though the steering wheel has been modified by the new owner.

As late as April 1975, Walter Wolf took delivery of this Miura SV,
number 5092. The car was built from spares three years after the
Miura production stopped.

Lamborghini has a large restoration shop where customer cars can be restored to original specifications. Here a Miura S, number 4088, is being rebuilt.

The small sports car firm AMS Autoracing, in Sasso Marconi near Bologna, built this monocoque sports car using a Miura engine. The car is now in Germany and for sale.

Photographed in New York some years ago, the Sonata by Enzo Stuardi. The car was based on the Miura and, though we should not fight about taste, to me it is the all-time ugly car.

Giotto Bizzarrini built this sports car using a Miura engine and transmission in 1966. The car was called P 538 and could also be had with a Chevrolet Corvette engine. One Lamborghini-powered car was built and two or three with Corvette units. In 1983, Bizzarrini builds replicas with Miura engines.

Lambo Motors, a Swiss Lamborghini dealer, built this Spider from a Miura S, number 4808, and had it for sale on the Lamborghini stand at the 1980 Geneva motor show.

This special was built by the French expert, now a Lamborghini dealer, Edmond Ciclet, for the 1971 Tour de France where the car was driven by Thierry Gore. The engine was tuned by Bob Wallace and had 360 hp at 8200 rpm. The differential came out of a Marzal and the car stood on 9- and 12-inch wheels. The Ferrari collector Pierre Bardinon tested the car on his private track and lapped in better times than with his Ferrari 250 LM.

CHAPTER 5

JOTA

Next to building replica Miura Spiders, it has become a fashion, especially in Europe, to "Jotanize" old Miuras. To make this new verb understandable you should know that the Lamborghini factory built one, and only one, car called the Jota. (Jota = J from the Appendix J rules of the FIA). This car was a hobby car for Bob Wallace who made it at the factory on Sundays and after work hours. The car was built on chassis 5084 in 1970, and was used for many experiments by Wallace. Basically the car was, of course, a Miura, but very little of the standard chassis or body was used. Avional was used where possible, on the doors, hood, dashboard, firewall and floor pan. The side-windows were made of plastic and were of the sliding type. The suspension was more like that of a racing car than of a Miura. The car stood on nine- and twelve-inch Campagnolo magnesium wheels fitted with Dunlop racing tires. Of course, Wallace took care of the engine, too. He raised the compression ratio to 11.5:1, and a dry-sump lubrication system was fitted. With an output of 440 hp at 8500 rpm the car, which was 350 kg (770 lb.) lighter than the ordinary Miura, had a top speed of 300 honest km/h (186 mph). In 1971 the car was sold and one year later totaled by an Italian count near Milano.

On special request, the factory rebuilt four Miuras to look like the Jota, but they did not have the same technical components, such as dry-sump lubrication, special suspension and so on. They probably had the numbers 4683, 4860, 4990 and 5113. These "official" factory-converted cars are certainly worth more money than ordinary Miuras, but since then, and even now, many Miura owners have rebuilt their cars to look like Jotas, which in my opinion is a shame and reduces the value of the car.

The one and only real Jota, photographed in front of the factory in 1970. Most of the body was made in Avional.

Hubert Hahne, Lamborghini dealer in Germany, had a Miura SV,
number 4860, rebuilt by the factory to look like the Jota.

Another of the four factory replicas went to Port au Prince, Haiti.
It carried chassis number 4990.

In November 1975 German Heinz E. Steber brought his Miura (3781) to the factory to have it Jotanized. The man in charge, Sen. Remo Vecci, did not like the idea at all, but accepted at last, as "money does not stink." It took the factory five months to do the job. The car had alloy fenders, a Countach spoiler, special wheels made by BBS, special Recaro seats, Koni racing shocks, an open exhaust, special camshafts and carburetors and Girling racing brakes from a 917 Porsche. The car is now with a collector in Japan.

CHAPTER 6

MARZAL

In addition to the two-seater Miura, Lamborghini wanted a new four-passenger car, fast and comfortable, for customers who had a family or needed occasional seats. Bertone built such a car in 1966 and showed it early in 1967 at the Geneva show. It was called the Marzal (another fighting bull) and it had a six-cylinder engine—half of a Miura engine—fitted transversely behind the rear axle. Even Lamborghini found the car too futuristic and did not accept the prototype for production. Bertone still has the car and, therefore, it is not likely that you will ever be able to buy it. The car was fully drivable as was demonstrated by Prince Rainier and Princess Grace of Monaco, who drove it as a pace car during the 1967 Monaco Grand Prix.

Model	**TP 200 Marzal**
Introduced	1966 Geneva motor show
Number built	1
Production years	1966
Engine	6 in-line
Bore x stroke in mm	82 x 62
Displacement in cc	1965
Valve operation	Double overhead camshafts
Compression ratio	9.2:1
Carburetion	3 Weber twin-throats
Bhp	175 at 6800 rpm
Chassis & Drivetrain	
Clutch	Single dry-plate, hydraulically operated
Transmission	Five-speed, all-synchromesh
Rear suspension	Independent, coil springs and telescopic shock absorbers
Front suspension	Independent, coil springs and telescopic shock absorbers
Frame	Tubular
General	
Wheelbase mm/in.	2620/102.1
Track, front mm/in.	1480/57.7
rear mm/in.	1480/57.7
Brakes	Girling discs
Tire size, front and rear	205-14
Body builder	Bertone
Overall height mm/in.	1080/42.1
Dry weight kg/lb.	1200/2640

Bertone's young styling chief, Marcello Gandini, lengthened a Miura chassis by 12 cm (4.5 in.), put a six-cylinder engine (half of a Miura V-12) transversely behind the rear axle—and created a four-seater Lamborghini.

The Marzal was even too much for Sig. Lamborghini—he could
not believe that he could sell such a futuristic car.

Many of the lines of the Marzal were to be found again on the later production car, the Espada.

CHAPTER 7
ESPADA

★★★

At the 1968 Geneva motor show Lamborghini introduced his first full four-seater car, the Espada. The line up now offered a two-seater Miura, the 2+2 Islero (presented at the same show), and this family sports car named for the sword carried by the matador with which he tries to kill the bull.

The first production Espada, shown in Geneva, carried the complex steering wheel of the Marzal, though following cars had a different design. Bertone even built a prototype with gull-wing doors as on the Marzal, but this idea was given up.

The Espada was, at that time, the fastest four-seater production car. Lamborghini had been right with his "family car"—demand was large. More than 1,200 have been built and in 1982 Ing. Giulio Alfieri, then director of Lamborghini, told me he regretted that the car was not in production anymore, as he was convinced he could still sell it.

The first Espadas were heavy steering, but power steering became optional on the second-series cars and standard on the third version, along with air conditioning. To get more space inside the car, the chassis, built by the small firm Marchesi (no longer from tubes, as used on the earlier Lamborghini models, but now as a platform), got a wheelbase of 2,650 cm, 10 cm longer (1,033.5/3.9) in.) than that of the Islero. With a track of 1,490 mm (58.1 in.) the car was very wide, and looked even wider because of the low roof lines of 1,185 mm (45.2 in.).

The second-series Espada, produced in 1969, had a new dash design and a more powerful engine (with a compression ratio of 10.7:1 instead of 9.8:1), giving 350 bhp at 7500 rpm instead of 325 at 6500. This engine was called the S-version on other Lamborghinis, but not mentioned on the Espada.

The third and last version had another different dashboard layout and an optional sunroof and Chrysler automatic transmission. For the American market the Espada had heavy black bumpers to meet safety regulations. Of course, the engines for this market were "clean" too.

The early Espadas had magnesium wheels, as used on the Islero, Miura and Jarama.

Dr. Urs Blum, the Swiss representative of the International Lamborghini Club, had this gearshift gate installed by the factory, which is always open to special requests. This Espada has chassis number 7825.

Two detail pictures of David Gamret's 1970 Espada. Note the different-styled steering wheel.

An early Espada ready for a crash test. This photograph was taken in October 1970.

Model . . . . **Espada**
Introduced . . . . 1968 Geneva motor show
Number built . . . . 1217 (no. 7001-9900)
Production years 1968-78
Engine . . . . V-12 60°
Bore x stroke in mm . . . . 82 x 62
Displacement in cc 3929
Valve operation . . . . . Double overhead camshafts on
each bank of cylinders
Compression ratio 10.7:1
Carburetion . . . . . . 6 twin-throat Webers, 40 DCOE 20
Bhp . . . . 350 at 7500 rpm
Chassis & Drivetrain
Clutch . . . . . . Single dry-plate, hydraulically operated
Transmission . . . . Five-speed, all-synchromesh
Rear suspension . . . . . . Independent, coil springs and
telescopic shock absorbers
Axle ratio 11/45
Front suspension . . . . . Independent, coil springs and
telescopic shock absorbers

Frame . . . . Integral chassis/body
General
Wheelbase mm/in 2650/103.4
Track, front mm/in 1490/58
rear mm/in 1490/58
Brakes . . . . Girling ventilated discs
Tire size, front and rear 205-15
Wheels . . . . Campagnolo cast magnesium
Body builder . . . . Bertone
Fuel tank capacity . . . . 93 lit/24 gal
Engine oil capacity . . . . 14 lit/14.7 qt
Cooling system capacity . . . . 14 lit/14.7 qt
Overall length mm/in 4738/184.8
Overall width mm/in 1860/72.5
Overall height mm/in 1185/46.2
Dry Weight kg/lb 1625/3575
Top speed kmph/mph 250/155

The 325 hp engine of the Espada first series. Note the unusual
way the rear vent windows open.

The second version of the Espada had different, more modern looking magnesium wheels, this time fixed with five bolts. The engine power was raised to 350 hp at 7500 rpm by changing the compression ratio from 9.5 to 10.7:1. Here is a 1973 model, chassis number 8604.

If you compare the second-series Espada with an early car, you will note very few differences under the hood.

Bertone built one Espada with a glass roof. The car is now in the US owned by Michael Kollins.

A different steering wheel was fitted on the second-series Espada (here, chassis number 8604). By the way, did you know that the direction indicator switch is the same as on the Austin Mini 1000? This is true for all Lamborghinis with a V-12 engine, except for the Countachs.

A European-version Espada with small, round side-marker lights in the fenders.

Another one-off Espada was the V.I.P., which Bertone built f[...]
show purposes. It is unlikely that it will be offered for sale.

The first prototype of the Espada is still lying
behind the factory in the scrap yard. Perhaps
it will be restored one day.

The third and last version of the Espada had a modified dashboard and, of course, a different steering wheel again. At last the
defrosters had been modified, by using a Bosch ventilator (from
Mercedes), but now hardly any air came to the feet of the driver
and passenger. Here is Jim Hall's 1975 car.

For the 1978 Turin motor show the Italian coachbuilder Frua created this four-door car on an early Espada chassis, number 18224. The car was shown again at the Geneva show two years later. It is now owned by a German, but is registered in Switzerland.

CHAPTER 8
ISLERO

★★

The Islero was probably introduced at the wrong moment: at the same 1968 Geneva show as the Espada. If one compares their body styling it will be clear why the Islero remained in the shadows of the Bertone car.

When Carrozzeria Touring went out of business, Lamborghini found the small coachbuilder Marazzi from Varese willing to design and build a new 2+2 as a successor for the 400 GT 2+2, which was getting old-fashioned.

The Islero was named after the most famous Spanish bull. This bull killed the famous matador Manuel Rodriguez August 28, 1947, and is still a legend.

The car had the mechanics of the 400 GT 2+2, but was 11.5 cm (4.5 in.) shorter and 65 kg (143 lb.) lighter, which made it really fast. Top speeds of 260 real km/h (161 mph) were measured, and one kilometer (.62 mile) could be covered from a standing start in twenty-five seconds. Still, the car was very comfortable and flexible to drive. One could drive with 1500 rpm in fifth gear and then accelerate to top speed without any protest from the engine. The interior was modernized and there was more head room for the rear passengers than in the 400 2+2.

After the summer holidays of 1969 the Islero could be had with a stronger engine (350 hp at 7500 rpm versus 340 at 7000) and this model was called the Islero S. It was not just the engine performance that was changed; the car went through a lot of facelifts, too. Air outlets were built on the sides of the front fenders and the air intake on the hood was enlarged. The fenders were widened a bit so that bigger tires could be fitted, and fog lights underneath the bumper were standard.

The upper part of the windshield was darkened and the rest of the windows were of tinted glass, with the rear window heater offered as standard equipment. The interior was taken care of, too. The front seats had higher backrests and the rear seat was separated into two seats now with an armrest between them. The car had, like the earlier Islero, the magnesium wheels as fitted on the Miura; though the Borrani wire wheels used on the 400 GT 2+2 would also fit.

The Islero and its S-version are still inexpensive compared to other Lamborghinis, but they are cars that can give a lot of pleasure.

This Islero was built in June 1968 and has the chassis number 6150.

The four-liter V-12 fills up the engine compartment.

The license plate holders show that the car runs in Switzerland, where one can have two cars with one set of plates, paying taxes and insurance for only one.

The lines of the car are badly disturbed when the headlights are in use. Fortunately, this happens only in the dark!

Model	400 GT Islero, Islero S
Introduced	1968 Geneva motor show
Number built	125 and 100 (no. 6000-6375 and 6381-6671)
Production years	1968 and 1969
Engine	V-12 60°
Bore x stroke in mm	82 x 62
Displacement in cc	3929
Valve operation	Double overhead camshafts on each bank of cylinders
Compression ratio	10.5:1 and 10.8:1
Carburetion	6 twin-throat Webers, 40 DCOE 20
Bhp	350 at 7500

Chassis & Drivetrain

Clutch	Single dry-plate, hydraulically operated
Transmission	Five-speed, all-synchromesh
Rear suspension	Independent, coil springs and telescopic shock absorbers
Axle ratio	11/45
Front suspension	Independent, coil springs and telescopic shock absorbers
Frame	Load-carrying body

General

Wheelbase mm/in.	2550/99.5
Track, front mm/in.	1380/53.8
rear mm/in.	1380/53.8
Brakes	Girling discs
Tire size, front and rear	205 VR 15
Wheels	Campagnolo, cast magnesium
Body builder	Marazzi of Milano
Fuel tank capacity	80 lit/21 gal
Engine oil capacity	14 lit/14.7
Cooling system capacity	16 lit/16.8
Overall length mm/in.	4525/176.5
Overall width mm/in.	1730/67.5
Overall height mm/in.	1300/50.7
Dry weight kg/lb	1315/2893
Top speed kmph/mph	250/155

The Islero's interior; the rear seat was in one piece. The later S-version had divided backrests.

Rob Fair's 1969 Islero, chassis number 6198. The air vents in the front fenders are not standard on this model, but look professionally made.

The pop-up headlights of the Islero are electrically operated. Here is an S-version, chassis number 6664.

The Islero S with chassis number 6671 was the last to leave the factory on April 15, 1970.

CHAPTER 9

JARAMA

★★★

In 1969 the last Islero S was built; but at the Geneva motor show of 1970, the factory introduced a new 2+2, the Jarama—named after the Spanish district famous for breeding fighting bulls.

The car was designed by Bertone, but Marazzi, a former employee of Touring, built the bodies. Again, a platform chassis was used and the mechanical part of the chassis was very much the same as on the Espada, though the wheelbase was 270 mm (10.5 in.) shorter than on the four-seater. Still, the car was heavy with its 1,540 kg (3,388 lb.) and, therefore, not so fast as the other Lamborghinis. This, plus the fact that strong competition came from the Maserati Indy introduced the year before, did not make the car a big hit.

There were 177 Jaramas built and sold between 1970 and 1973—not too bad a figure when one remembers the poor reviews the car had in the automotive press. *Road & Track* wrote: "A Lamborghini is a Lamborghini, but this one wasn't up to the usual standard."

In 1972 a faster version, the Jarama 400 GTS, was introduced in Geneva. Like the other S-versions it had more horsepower and now an acceptable top speed—the 260 km/h (161.2 mph) the factory had earlier claimed for the first version. The interior was revised and more leg room for the rear-seat passengers was created by modifying the rear seats. A large air intake, almost covering the width of the hood, prevented overheating of the engine (a problem the earlier cars had), and air outlets between the front wheel and the door were fitted. Of course the car got the bolt-on wheels that were in fashion on Lamborghinis at that time, replacing the knock-off type.

The Jarama S could also be had with a Targa-type roof, but this option was not sold very often. A less desirable option was the Chrysler Torqueflite automatic gearbox, which was fine for an American engine, but not for a Lamborghini V-12.

The jig around which the Jarama was built.

A 1970 Jarama. This car is not a European version, which had round indicator lights in the front fenders.

The trunk of the Jarama had a capacity of 250 liters.

Lamborghini Development Engineer Bob Wallace, now running a restoration shop in the US, built this special Jarama GTS. The car had lighter body panels, a roll-over cage, spoilers and a fuel filler cap through the rear window. The car was a personal toy for Wallace and was never entered in a race. It now belongs to a French collector.

A Jarama seen from the rear at the 1971 Geneva show. The chassis number of this car is 10068.

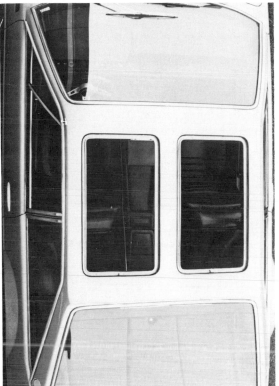

Model	400 GT (GTS) Jarama
Introduced	1970 (1972) Geneva motor show
Number built	177 and 150 (no. 10.000-10.350) and 10.352-10.660)
Production years	1970-73 and 1973-76
Engine	V-12 60°
Bore x stroke in mm	82 x 62
Displacement in cc	3929
Valve operation	Double overhead camshafts on each bank of cylinders
Compression ratio	10.7:1
Carburetion	6 twin-throat Webers, 40 DCOE 20-21
Bhp	350 (365) at 7500 rpm

Chassis & Drivetrain

Clutch	Single dry-plate, hydraulically operated
Transmission	Five-speed, all-synchromesh
Rear suspension	Independent, coil springs and telescopic shock absorbers
Axle ratio	11/45
Front suspension	Independent, coil springs and telescopic shock absorbers
Frame	Integral chassis/body

General

Wheelbase mm/in.	2380/92.8
Track, front mm/in.	1490/58
rear mm/in.	1490/58
Brakes	Girling ventilated discs
Tire size, front and rear	215-15 (215-70-15)
Wheels	Campagnolo cast magnesium
Body builder	Marazzi
Fuel tank capacity	100 lit/26.25 gal
Engine oil capacity	14 lit/14.7 qt
Cooling system capacity	14 lit/14.7 qt
Overall length mm/in.	4485/174.7
Overall width mm/in.	1820/71
Overall height mm/in.	1190/46.4
Dry weight kg/lb.	1540 (1460)/3388(3212)
Top speed kmph/mph	245 (260)/152(161)

The interior of Mike Stevenson's 1972 Jarama. This car has a Targa-type roof. One or both panels can be removed.

The Jarama S, recognizeable by the big air intake on the hood
and the outlets in the front fenders. The time of Borrani wire wheels
was over as the new magnesium wheels were bolted with five
bolts.

In February 1974, Ferruccio Lamborghini drove this Jarama S, chassis number 10418. By the way, did you know the clutch disc of a Jaguar XJ 6 fits a Jarama and that the Jarama and Espada Series III taillights are the same as on a Pantera?

CHAPTER 10
URRACO

★★ P 250
★★ P 200
★★★ P 300

"The noise in the cabin sounded like a recording I have that was taped at a point a couple inches behind Graham Hill's helmet as he drove a BRM around the Grand Prix circuit at Monte Carlo—though most of the gear changes sounded better." That was how L.J.K. Setright described the noise in a Urraco in *Motor*, of May 11, 1974. I never heard the gramophone record, but he must have exaggerated. Still, the car is noisy and louder than one should expect in a family car, which the Uracco was designed to be.

Porsche sells a lot of cars in Italy (strange); plus when the Ferrari/Fiat Dino 206 came on the market in the late sixties Ferruccio Lamborghini thought the time ripe for a competing car. It should be a four-seater, but still the engine should be in the rear and in front of the rear axle for better handling than a Porsche. The only solution was to build the engine transversely behind the rear seat; but a six-cylinder, as in the Marzal, was too long and a four-cylinder not "enough" Lamborghini. So a V-8 was constructed. The engine became, for Lamborghini standards, a rather simple unit: two blocks of four cylinders at an angle of ninety degrees, and one overhead camshaft per bank of cylinders, driven by an external-toothed belt. As the combustion chambers were in the piston heads, flat Heron-type heads were used. With a compression ratio of 10.5:1 the 2462.9 cc engine had an output of 220 hp at 7800 rpm.

The chassis was of the platform type and for the first time a MacPherson strut suspension was used, fore and aft, on a high performance car. Bertone managed to design and build a good-looking car, certainly a difficult task with these specifications. The car was introduced at the Turin motor show in October 1970 as the P 250 Urraco (P = posteriore, rear, 250; or 2.5 liters; a urraco is a young fighting bull) but social and political problems, not unusual in Italy, prevented fabrication until 1972. When the production of the P 250 was stopped in 1976, 520 cars had been built.

For the American market the P 111 was designed, basically the same as the other Urracos, but carrying heavy black bumpers and indicator lights in the sides of the fenders. Ing. Stanzani had many problems getting the engine "clean" for the US. He tried fuel injection but ended up with Solex carburetors, as Porsche used on its American version cars. The engine performance dropped badly, though, from 220 to 180 hp, so that the car could not compete with the Porsches, except in road holding.

The American Lamborghini importer had promised to take a large quantity of Urracos (and 800 units were built) but now, of course, he

Two Bertone photographs of the P 250 Urraco. It must have been a difficult task to design a four-seater car, with the engine in front of the rear wheels and a total length of only 4,250 mm.

drew back, leaving the factory with too many spares. A way of using them was discovered in a small-version Urraco, the P 200 with a 1994 cc engine, which appeared at the 1974 Turin show. The car was built for the Italian market, since cars with two-liter (or less) engines have inviting tax reductions. Sixty-Six cars of this two-liter type were sold.

At the same 1974 Turin show a three-liter version was introduced, the P 300. With its four overhead camshafts and 260 hp this was a *real* Lamborghini again. About 200 P 300's were built before the factory was forced to stop producing them due to financial difficulties. These V-8 engines were of a good quality, though not so reliable as the V-12, where 100,000 miles without any major engine work was no exception.

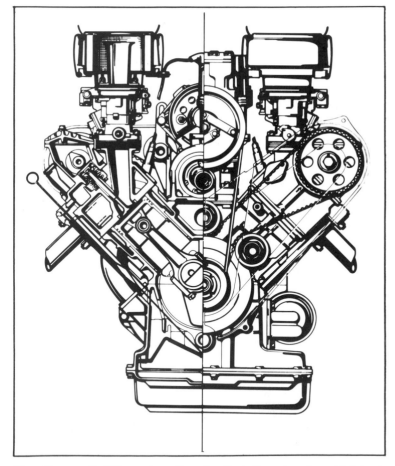

The Urraco P 250 engine. For the first time Lamborghini had built an engine with "only" one overhead camshaft per bank of cylinders.

The distributor of the Urraco was poorly located, as it tended to give trouble when the engine was really hot.

Model	P 250 Urraco
Introduced	1970 Turin motor show
Number built	520 (no. 15.000-15.988)
Production years	1972-76
Engine	V-8 90° transverse mid engine
Bore x stroke in mm	86 x 53
Displacement in cc	2462
Valve operation	1 overhead camshaft on each bank of cylinders
Compression ratio	10.5:1
Carburetion	Twin-throat Webers, 40 IDF 1
Bhp	220 at 7500 rpm

Chassis & Drivetrain

Clutch	Single dry-plate, hydraulically operated
Transmission	Five-speed, all-synchromesh
Rear suspension	Independent, coil springs and telescopic shock absorbers
Axle ratio	16/68
Front suspension	Independent, coil springs and telescopic shock absorbers
Frame	Integral chassis/body

General

Wheelbase mm/in.	2450/95.5
Track, front mm/in.	1460/57
rear mm/in.	1460/57
Brakes	Girling ventilated discs
Tire size, front and rear	205-14
Wheels	Campagnolo cast magnesium
Body builder	Bertone
Fuel tank capacity	80 lit/21 gal
Engine oil capacity	7.5 lit/7.9 qt
Cooling system capacity	12 lit/12.6 qt
Overall length mm/in.	4250/165.8
Overall width mm/in.	1760/68.6
Overall height mm/in.	1160/45.2
Dry weight kg/lb.	1100/2420
Top speed kmph/mph	230/142.6

The Urraco had flat Heron heads, the combustion chambers were cut in the heads of the pistons.

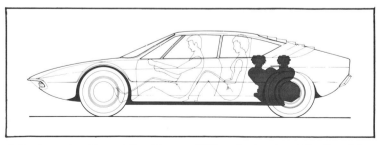

A Bertone drawing of the Urraco. Without a backrest for the driver's seat, another person could sit behind it. In practice this was impossible as the car was only suitable for three adults or two adults and two children.

Very early P 250's had this type of dashboard with three control lights on the right, instead of four behind the steering wheel.

Bertone made the bodies for the Urraco, here a P 250 photographed in 1974. When Bertone shipped the "car" to Lamborghini it was completely assembled, upholstered and painted, so that the Lamborghini factory installed only the suspension and power-train.

The P 250 engine with belt-driven camshafts. Although the gearbox and differential were blocked with the V-8 engine, the unit was short enough to be placed transversely in the car. It was difficult to engage first gear in the Urraco gearbox.

Three views of the 1971 production P 250 as photographed at the Geneva show.

Shown here is a 1973 P 250 with chassis number 15354 and German registrations.

The P 250 Urraco, here a 1974 model with chassis number 15494,
can be recognized by the divided-looking trunk lid.

Model. . . . . **P 200 Urraco**
Introduced . . . . 1974 Turin motor show
Number built . . . . 66 (no. 20.000-20.600)
Production years 1975-77
Engine . . . . V-8 90° transverse, mid engine
Bore x stroke in mm . . . . 77.4 x 53
Displacement in cc 1994
Valve operation . . . . 1 overhead camshaft on
each bank of cylinders
Compression ratio 8.6:1
Carburetion . . . . 4 twin-throat Webers, IDF 40
Bhp . . . . 182 at 7500 rpm

Chassis & Drivetrain
Clutch . . . . . . Single dry-plate, hydraulically operated
Transmission . . . . Five-speed, all-synchromesh
Rear suspension . . . . . . Independent, coil springs and
telescopic shock absorbers
Axle ratio 14/35
Front suspension . . . . Independent, coil springs
and telescopic shock absorbers

Frame . . . . Integral chassis/body
General
Wheelbase mm/in. 2450/95.5
Track, front mm/in. 1450/56.5
rear mm/in. 1470/57.3
Brakes . . . . Girling ventilated discs
Tire size, front and rear . . . . 195/70 VR 14 and
205/70 VR 14
Wheels . . . . Campagnolo cast magnesium 7.5x14J
Body builder . . . . Bertone
Fuel tank capacity . . . . 80 lit/21 gal
Engine oil capacity . . . . 7.5 lit/7.9 qt
Cooling system capacity . . . . 12 lit/12.6 qt
Overall length mm/in. 4250/165.8
Overall width mm/in. 1760/68.6
Overall height mm/in. 1160/45.2
Dry weight kg/lb. 1250/2750
Top speed kmph/mph 260/161.2

The engine of the Urraco P 200 was built for the Italian market, where the road tax for cars with a capacity of less than 2000 cc is much less than for bigger cars.

A German-registered Urraco 3000.

Model	**P 300 Urraco**
Introduced	1974 Turin motor show
Number built	190 (no. 30.000-30.200)
Production years	1975-79
Engine	V-8 90° transverse, mid engine
Bore x stroke in mm	86 x 64.5
Displacement in cc	2995.8
Valve operation	Double overhead camshafts on each bank of cylinders
Compression ratio	10.5:1
Carburetion	4 twin-throat Webers, 40 DCNF
Bhp	265 at 7800 rpm

Chassis & Drivetrain

Clutch	Single dry-plate, hydraulically operated
Transmission	Five-speed, all-synchromesh
Rear suspension	Independent, coil springs and telescopic shock absorbers
Axle ratio	14/35
Front suspension	Independent, coil springs and telescopic shock absorbers

Frame	Integral chassis/body

General

Wheelbase mm/in.	2450/95.5
Track, front mm/in.	1450/56.5
rear mm/in.	1470/57.3
Brakes	Girling ventilated discs
Tire size, front and rear	195/70 VR 14 and 205/70 VR 14
Wheels	Campagnolo cast magnesium 7.5x14J
Body builder	Bertone
Fuel tank capacity	80 lit/21 gal
Engine oil capacity	7.5 lit/7.9 qt
Cooling system capacity	15 lit/15.8 qt
Overall length mm/in.	4250/165.8
Overall width mm/in.	1760/68.6
Overall height mm/in.	1160/45.2
Dry weight kg/lb.	1280/2816
Top speed kmph/mph	250/155

One of the prototypes of the Urraco is still lying behind the factory, waiting for someone to restore it. Note the four headlights.

The instrument panel of the P 111 (bottom) was the same as that
of the P 300 (top), but different in layout from the P 250.

Though the factory never made a "racing car" this P 300 was modified by Lamborghini. It was never seen on a track, though.

★★★★★ LP 500
★★★ LP 400
★★★★ LP 400 S
★★★★ LP 5000 S
★★★★★ LP 5000
Quattrovalvole
★★★★★ 25th Anniversary

CHAPTER 11

COUNTACH

When the last and best version of the Miura, the SV, was introduced to the public at the 1971 Geneva motor show, the car was hardly noticed. The reason was the simultaneous introduction of an extremely futuristic car which would follow the Miura line. The Countach (an untranslatable expression from the Piedmont dialect, used when seeing something marvelous) LP 500 (Longitudinal Posteriore 5 Litri, or longitudinal-rear five liters) had a V-12 engine enlarged from 3929 to 4971 cc and fitted in front of the rear axle with the gearbox between the two seats. The power was taken off the gearbox to the differential, which was mounted between the rear wheels, by a shaft that ran through the entire length of the engine. Thus, the car's weight ratio was superb. The power unit was very light and metals like magnesium were used where possible.

The chassis was built from tubes strengthened by steel plating but the bodywork was made in steel. The body, of course, was the most interesting. Designed and built by Bertone, the car was extremely wide (1,870 mm, 73 in.) and wedge shaped (1,030 mm, 40 in., high) like earlier Bertone show cars (Carabo, Lancia Stratos). But there was a difference This time it was not meant to be just a show car; it would actually be produced in this futuristic form.

The doors of the Countach opened as they had on the Carabo: vertically, by hydraulic jacks. The interior of this prototype looked like a space ship with control lights, an illuminated chassis plan showing possible faults and so on. As the rear view was zero, this car sported a periscope mirror.

Only one LP 500 was built and there is no hope for finding it; as it was destroyed in the crash test at MIRA (Motor Industry Research Association) in England.

LP 400

At the 1973 Geneva motor show, Lamborghini proudly presented the Countach LP 400, the production version of the 1971 LP 500. The production car looked very much like the LP 500, but there were differences. Bob Wallace had a different chassis made by the Modena firm Marchesi (which is still building them for Lamborghini), and now the body was made of aluminum. To save as much weight as possible Gleverbel glass was manufactured in Belgium and magnesium replaced heavier metals in many cases. As the engine in the first car tended to overheat, the production car had extra air boxes in front of relocated radiators. NACA air inlets starting in the door panels also helped to keep the engine cool.

Only one Countach LP 500 was built for the 1971 Geneva motor show. The car no longer exists. Note the periscope mirror in the middle of the roof.

Extra little side-windows were made in the doors and the car had new, less futuristic taillights. American Stewart-Warner instruments replaced the Italian ones and the trouble-finding diagram had disappeared.

On the first production LP 400's many parts, such as the four hub carriers, were made of magnesium, but later cars had these items made of aluminum. The engine capacity became four liters now; first, because the five-liter had given some problems and, second, because many of the production four-liter engines could now be used. Fichtel & Sachs provided the aluminum clutch, which had also been used in the 917 Porsches. Two six-plug Marelli distributors replaced the twelve-plug unit of the LP 500.

The 1973 Geneva show car was used by Bob Wallace for test runs. For the Paris show of that same year a second car was built, again completely by Lamborghini, as Bertone did not make the bodies for the Countach. The demand for the car was growing and orders from importers kept coming in. Still, the first car that went to a customer was the one exhibited at the 1974 Geneva show. Much time was wasted, during which many Miuras could have been sold.

LP 400 S

Walter Wolf's personal Countachs always had something special; and when the new Pirelli P-7 tires came out he had his car immediately fitted with them, which needed some readjusting of the suspension.

Many Countach owners followed and so a new version, the Countach S, took shape. This new model became available early in 1978. The engine did not change, but mechanical improvements were made. With the P-7 tires, the location points for springs and shock absorbers were changed and a new antiroll bar on the front end made the car more rigid. The brake system was modified now having 300 mm (11.7 in.) discs on the front and 284 mm (11.1 in.) on the rear wheels. Instead of Girling calipers German ATE's were fitted. The wheel arches were widened so that new wheels, as seen on the Bravo, could be fitted with 205/50 VR 15 Pirelli P-7 tires on the front and 345/35 VR 15's on the rear wheels. These modifications meant that the hub carriers had to be redesigned on all four wheels.

In the fall of 1979 the S-version got bigger instruments with a speedometer marked in km/h and mph, which made it rather difficult to read. An adjustable rear wing—one of the Wolf modifications—could be had as an option.

Hubert Hahne, who had a finger in Lamborghini's financial affairs at the time, showed a "turbocharged" Countach engine at the 1979 Frankfurt motor show, but the construction looked so primitive that I do not think it ever worked. This modification was made in Germany and not by the factory.

At the 1982 Geneva show a Lamborghini Countach 5000 was presented, for those drivers that needed a little more engine power.

By the time of this writing, spring 1983, a total of 500+ Countachs has been built, with the latest chassis number being ZA9C 00500 DLA 12560. Although, at this moment, the car is not legal for the US, there are probably more Countachs in America than in the rest of the world

The production cars each had a four-liter engine instead of this five-liter unit used in the LP 500 prototype.

Bob Wallace road tested the LP 500 on the Autostrade. The pieces of wool glued to the body will give information about the aerodynamic shape of the body.

together. These cars were modified by specialists or imported for show purposes. For Sheldon Brooks in Minnesota, the factory built a car conforming to the US specifications, but the huge bumpers made it the ugliest car ever built by Lamborghini. The American importers seem to have found better ways to get the cars through inspections.

If you ever consider buying a car in Europe, for use in the US, part of a letter written to me by Trefor Thomas of Lamborghini of North America might interest you: "On any car which is more than five years old and is imported by an individual, no EPA Emission Control Equipment is required at present [i.e., at the time of this writing, any car built prior to December 31, 1978, will be emissions exempt].

"As far as safety equipment is concerned, on Countaches built prior to November 1978 must be modified as follows:

Head lamps must be sealed beams

Side marker lights and reflectors—DOT approved glass all around

American specification seat belts

Seat belt warning light and buzzer

MPH speedometer

Variable lighting for heater controls

All electric switches must have the correct identification symbols

Ignition lock has to be changed

Secondary return spring has to be installed on the accelerator control

Door intrusion beams must be installed

"There are probably a few other minor things, but most of the companies who undertake conversions to meet American specifications know what these are.

"On cars built after November 1, 1978, a 5 mile per hour bumper system, front and rear, is required.

"On the new LP 400 and 400 S, Full Emission Controls are required, a somewhat expensive and elaborate system of controls comprising air injection pumps, four catalytic converters, air diverter valve, and full fuel vapor recovery system has to be installed. On the LP 500 S, we have to convert the car to fuel injection of the CIS type with oxygen sensors and feed back closed-loop system to meet the more stringent regulations now in existence and to form the basis of the U.S. legal 5 litre car to be built by the factory."

LP 500

In addition to the LP 400 S, which remained in production, the Lamborghini factory offered a Countach with a five-liter engine in 1982. The car again was introduced at the Geneva show, where so many new Lamborghini models saw first light.

The cars looked similar except for the door panels, which had been modified, and technical differences to be found. In the engine, parts were replaced, the gear ratios were revised and the front suspension was changed. An air pump was now fitted, and inside the car some of the switches were replaced for safety reasons.

The interior of the original LP 500. On the diagram one could see if something did not work properly. This diagram did not appear in production cars.

Model	**LP 500 Countach**
Introduced	1971 Geneva motor show
Number built	1
Production years	1971
Engine	V-12 60°
Bore x stroke in mm	85 x 73
Displacement in cc	4971
Valve operation	Double overhead camshafts on each bank of cylinders
Compression ratio	10.5:1
Carburetion	6 twin-throat Webers, 45 DCOE 96/97
Bhp	440 at 7400 rpm
Chassis & Drivetrain	
Clutch	Single dry-plate, hydraulically operated
Transmission	Five-speed, all-synchromesh
Rear suspension	Independent, coil springs and telescopic shock absorbers
Axle ratio	11/45
Front suspension	Independent, coil springs and telescopic shock absorbers
Frame	Tubular
General	
Wheelbase mm/in.	2450/95.5
Track, front mm/in.	1500/58.5
rear mm/in.	1520/59.3
Brakes	Girling ventilated discs
Tire size, front and rear	205/70 VR 14 and 215/70 VR 14
Wheels	Campagnolo cast magnesium
Body builder	Bertone
Fuel tank capacity	2x70 lit/2x18.4 gal
Overall length mm/in.	4010/156.4
Overall width mm/in.	1870/72.9
Overall height mm/in.	1030/40.2
Dry weight kg/lb	1130/2486
Top speed kmph/mph	290/179.8

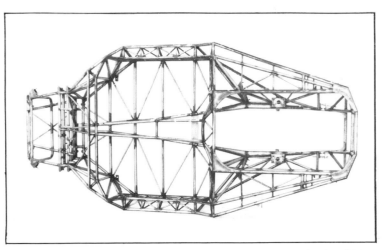

If you study the photograph of the Countach chassis, it will be clear that it needs a real expert to repair such a car after a crash.

When the Countach appeared to the public for the first time in 1971 nobody thought this machine would ever go into production. It was too futuristic to be a usable piece of transportation and now, even after so many years, one gets this same impression. Of course the Countach is no car to go shopping in, but then it was never built to be anything else than a rich person's toy.

And a toy it can be. The car handles beautifully and steers around corners as if it runs on rails. Even though the windshield is raked so steeply, visibility is good. Problems arise only when parking the car, as the front end of the car cannot be seen. Looking to the rear is different thing and backing up needs some practice! The best way to see is to open the door and sit on the doorstep.

The sound the engine makes is for car nuts only, especially at higher rpm when it starts screaming. Of course it needs an experienced driver to handle the car as it is tempting to drive very fast. In case of an accident, it is not the easiest car to get out of, though Lamborghini's test driver Valentino Balboni escaped through a side window when his car tipped over and started burning. Good for Valentino that he was not too big. . . .

There is a big difference in value between cars modified by a shop or by the factory. As mentioned before, the Lamborghini factory people always had an open ear for customers who wanted a little item changed or some modifications made to their cars; and they even went as far as making "replicas" of the Miura Jota for certain customers.

Walter Wolf was a different case. First, he was a friend of Sig. Lamborghini; second, he was a very good customer; and third, he gave the factory hope of being saved when times were really bad.

Wolf always had some special requests. Three special Countachs (after the Miura period) have been built for him. The first, a 1974 model, can be called a prototype of the Countach S—with a big wing on the rear, a reminder that Wolf also ran a Formula One racing team. As all Wolf cars, this one had a five-liter engine which he had on loan from the factory and which was removed when the car was sold (to be put into his next car). The first car had different spoilers and a steering wheel of the make "Personal F-1." The first Wolf Countach, a red one, was sold to someone in Japan.

LP 5000 Quattrovalvole

Enough is never enough. Even the world's most revered super car can be caught napping. Farrari's new-in-1984 Testarossa was indeed much "closer" to the Countach—too close for comfort. And so for 1985, Lamborghini launched the LP 5000 Quattrovalvole (or five-liter four-valve), actually 5167 cc, at the Geneva show and immediately "escaped" again. Reported horsepower and torque were both up on that of the Testarossa. Externally the car was much the same except for a bulging rear engine cover (both front and rear lids now in Kevlar), which hid six vertical downdraft 44DCNF Webers. New also was a ZF five-speed.

The compact Countach engine with the gearbox on the left and the differential on the right-hand side.

Note that the doors open vertically on the Countachs.

The first prototype ready for the 1973 Geneva Show. NACA ducts and big air intakes are for cooling air to the, now, vertically mounted water radiators. Note the difference between this and the 1971 show car.

110

The interior of the second prototype and the complex windshield wiper.

The third prototype, or second LP400, was shown to the public at the 1973 Paris show. The green-painted car had driving lights integrated in the alloy grille, and the parts of the door windows that could be opened had grown a bit.

Model	LP 400 Countach		Frame	Tubular
Introduced	1973 Geneva motor show		**General**	
Number built	150		Wheelbase mm/in.	2450/95.5
Production years	1974-78 (no. 112.0001-		Track, front mm/in.	1500/58.5
	112.0300)		rear mm/in.	1520/59.3
Engine	V-12 60°		Brakes	Girling ventilated discs
Bore x stroke in mm	82 x 62		Tire size, front and rear	205/70 x 14 and
Displacement in cc	3929			215/70 x 14
Valve operation	Double overhead camshafts on		Wheels	Campagnolo cast magnesium 7.5 and
	each bank of cylinders			9.5 JJ x 14

Model .... LP 400 Countach
Introduced .... 1973 Geneva motor show
Number built 150
Production years .... 1974-78 (no. 112.0001-
112.0300)
Engine .... V-12 60°
Bore x stroke in mm .... 82 x 62
Displacement in cc 3929
Valve operation .....Double overhead camshafts on
each bank of cylinders
Compression ratio 10.5:1
Carburetion .... 6 twin-throat Webers, 45 DCOE
96/97
Bhp .... 375 at 8000 rpm
Chassis & Drivetrain
Clutch ...... Single dry-plate, hydraulically operated
Transmission .... Five-speed, all-synchromesh
Rear suspension...... Independent, coil springs and
telescopic shock absorbers
Axle ratio................................. 11/45
Front suspension ..... Independent, coil springs and
telescopic shock absorbers

Frame .... Tubular
General
Wheelbase mm/in. 2450/95.5
Track, front mm/in. 1500/58.5
rear mm/in. 1520/59.3
Brakes .... Girling ventilated discs
Tire size, front and rear .... 205/70 x 14 and
215/70 x 14
Wheels .... Campagnolo cast magnesium 7.5 and
9.5 JJ x 14
Body builder .... Lamborghini
Fuel tank capacity .... 2x60 lit/2x16 gal
Engine oil capacity .... 17.5 lit/18.4 qt
Cooling system capacity .... 17 lit/17.8 qt
Overall length mm/in. 4140/161.5
Overall width mm/in. 1890/73.7
Overall height mm/in. 1070/41.7
Dry weight kg/lb. 1300/2860
Top speed kmph/mph 290/179.8

On the production cars the door windows were different. The window frames and "bumpers" were no longer made of aluminum. Here's a little tip: If you want to back up in a Countach you open the door and lean out the side of the car with your left hand on the wheel, and hold yourself in with your right hand.

The rear side windows of the Countach are just large enough to let light come in.

The Countach engine, photographed in 1975. On the right-hand side, the five-speed gearbox; on the left, the differential with the drive going through the sump.

The 205/50 VR 15 P 7 Pirelli tire looks lost under the fender of this S, number 112.1180.

For Sheldon Brooks, in Minnesota, the factory built a Countach S, to American specifications. The big bumpers, of course, ruined the line of the car.

The rear wing was an option available on the S series. Most cars were delivered with one. Here is number 112.1092.

At the 1980 Turin show Lamborghini had only a tiny stand with two Countach S's on display, a dark one and a white one.

The first-series Countach S still had a readable speedometer. The white bar on the right-hand side of the tunnel is for the passenger to hold onto. This is car number 112.1092, a 1980 model.

The second-series Countach had a completely new dashboard layout.

Model . . . . **Countach LP 400 S**	**Frame** . . . . Tubular
Introduced . . . . 1978 Geneva motor show	**General**
Number built . . . . 466 (no. 121.004-121.470)	Wheelbase mm/in. 2450/95.5
Production years 1978-82	Track, front mm/in. 1490/58
Engine . . . . V-12 60°	rear mm/in. 1605/62.5
Bore x stroke in mm . . . . 82 x 62	Brakes . . . . Girling ventilated discs
Displacement in cc 3929	Tire size, front and rear . . . . 205/50 VR-15 and
Valve operation . . . . . Double overhead camshafts on	345/35 VR-15 Pirelli P-7's
each bank of cylinders	Wheels . . . . . . Campagnolo magnesium 8.5 and 12 J.
Compression ratio 10.5:1	Body builder . . . . Designed by Bertone, built by
Carburetion . . . . . . 6 twin-throat Webers, DCOE 96-97	Lamborghini
Bhp . . . . 375 at 8000 rpm	Fuel tank capacity . . . . 2x60 lit/2x16 gal
Chassis & Drivetrain	Engine oil capacity . . . . 17.5 lit/18.4 qt
Clutch . . . . . . Single dry-plate, hydraulically operated	Cooling system capacity . . . . 17 lit/17.8 qt
Transmission . . . . Five-speed, all-synchromesh	Overall length mm/in. 4140/161.5
Rear suspension . . . . . . Independent, coil springs and	Overall width mm/in. 2000/78
telescopic shock absorbers	Overall height mm/in. 1070/41.7
Axle ratio 11/45	Dry weight kg/lb. 1360/2992
Front suspension . . . . . Independent, coil springs and	Top speed kmph/mph 290/179.8
telescopic shock absorbers	

The Countach S could be had without a rear wing, too, as this photograph, taken at the 1980 Turin show, proves. The rear window is of no use.

The dashboard of the five-liter Countach was similar to the second-series LP 400, but can be recognized by the switches on the console.

This 1982 Countach LP 5000 is white, inside and out.

Grinding the first coat of primer on a five-liter Countach.

Much time is spent with detailed handwork. Here is a specialist working on a 1982 Countach door.

This Countach LP 5000 was the official pace car for the 1982 Monaco Grand Prix.

In May 1982 Armin Johl took delivery of his new, black Countach 5000 or five-liter (chassis number 12.480). Members of the International Lamborghini Club were there to help him celebrate.

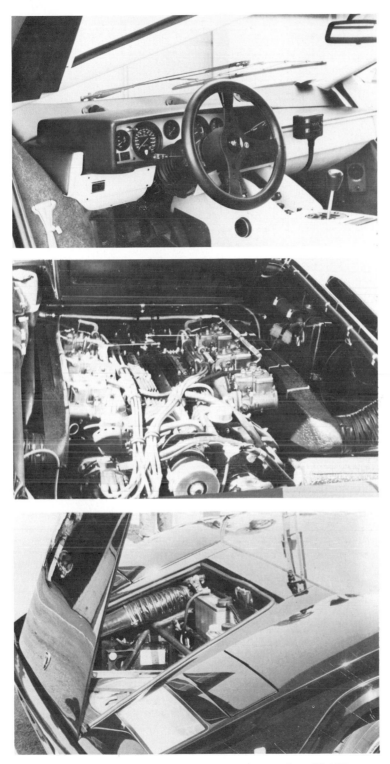

Details of Armin Johl's five-liter Countach, number 12.480.

The five-liter Countach engine with fuel injection as modified by
Lamborghini of North America in 1982.

The second Wolf Countach had the wing on the rear electrically
adjustable. The car was decorated with Wolf signets and Canadian
flags. This 1976 car is in Germany now.

These photographs, taken in May 1982, show a Countach LP 5000, chassis number 12.486, on the production line. The right-hand-drive car was built for a customer in Hong Kong. The black exterior looked very good with the white interior.

The Wolf cars had a special, F-1-type steering wheel with "Walter Wolf" engraved on it.

Walter Wolf's third "special" was the first Countach S built. He had his own five-liter engine and a double disc Borg & Beck F-1 clutch installed. The brakes, with the front to rear balance adjustable from the cockpit, had eight pistons per caliper. The car was shown at the 1978 Geneva show, without wing, but sporting Wolf hubcaps.

A rare photograph taken during a meeting of the international Lamborghini Owners Club in Germany: On the left, the Wolf Countach number 3 and on the far right, the Wolf car number 2.

Model	LP 5000S Countach
Introduced	1982 Geneva motor show
Number built	323
Production years	1982-85 (no. 12.472-12.795)
Engine	V-12 60°
Bore x stroke in mm	69 x 85.5
Displacement in cc	4754
Valve operation	Double overhead camshafts on each bank of cylinders
Compression ratio	9.2:1
Carburetion	6 twin-throat Webers. 45 DCOE
Bhp	375 at 7000 rpm

Chassis & Drivetrain

Clutch	Single dry-plate, hydraulically operated
Transmission	Five-speed, all-synchromesh
Rear suspension	Independent. coil springs and telescopic shock absorbers
Axle ratio	11/45
Front suspension	Independent. coil springs and telescopic shock absorbers
Frame	Tubular

General

Wheelbase mm/in.	2450/95.5
Track, front mm/in.	1492/58.2
rear mm/in.	1606/62.6
Brakes	ATE ventilated discs
Tire size, front and rear	205/50VR15 P7 and 345/35VR15 P7
Wheels	The first 20 cars were built with Campagnolo magnesium wheels. The later cars were equipped with wheels made by Ozzeta in electron.
Body builder	Lamborghini
Fuel tank capacity	2x60 lit/2x16 gal
Engine oil capacity	15 lit/15.75 qt
Cooling system capacity	16 lit/16.8 qt
Overall length mm/in.	4140/161.5
Overall width mm/in.	2000/78
Overall height mm/in.	1070/41.7
Dry Weight kg/lb	1480/3256
Top speed kmph/mph	294/182.3

For some people even a Countach S is not fast enough. Max Bobnar, a Swiss Lamborghini collector, had his car (number 112.1160)
equipped with two superchargers and now his engine has 520
hp at 6500 rpm. The car accelerates from 0-100 km/h (62 mph)
in 4.8 seconds and from 0-200 km/h (125 mph) in 16 seconds.

Model . . . . **Countach LP 5000 Quattrovalvole**	Frame . . . . .Tubular
Introduced . . . . .Geneva motor show 1985	**General**
Production years . . . . .1985-July 1988; 632 cars built	Wheelbase mm/in. 2500/97.5
Engine . . . . .V-12 60°, Type LP 112 D	Track, front mm/in. 1536/59.9
Bore × stroke in mm .85.5 × 75	rear mm/in. 1606/62.6
Displacement in cc 5167	Brakes . . . . .Ventilated discs
Valve operation . . . . .Double overhead cam-	Tire size, front and rear 225/50 VR 15 and
shafts on each bank of cylinders. Four	345/35 VR 15
valves per cylinder.	Wheels . . . . .Magnesium; front 8.5, rear 12
Compression ratio 9.5:1	Body builder . . . . .Lamborghini
Carburetion . . . . .6 twin-throat Webers, 44 DCNF	Fuel tank capacity . . . . .2 × 60 lit
Bhp . . . . .455 at 7000 rpm	Engine oil capacity .17 lit/17.9 qt
Chassis & Drivetrain	Cooling system capacity . . . . .17 lit/17.9 qt
Clutch . . . . .Single dry-plate, hydraulically	Overall length mm/in. .4140/161.5
operated	Overall width mm/in. 2000/78
Transmission . . . . .Five-speed, all-synchromesh	Overall height mm/in. .1070/41.7
Rear suspension . . . . .Independent, coil springs	Dry weight kg/lb 1490/3278
and telescopic shock absorbers	Top speed kmph/mph .300/186
Axle ratio 11/45	
Front suspension . . . . .Independent, coil springs	
and telescopic shock absorbers	

Bobnar's two Raja turbochargers and the three waste gate valves.

Lamborghini of North America put its own wings on the Countachs. They got through the inspections until the end of 1981. After September 1983 the model should be again legal for the US, though.

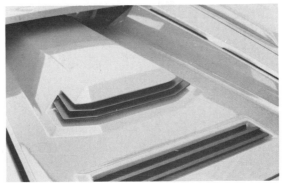

The carburetors of the Quattrovalvole are mounted vertically, asking for "bubbles" on the engine hood.

The 455 hp V-12 has a total of forty-eight valves.

Test driver Valentino Balboni back from a drive in a four-valve Countach, chassis number 12.876.

25th Anniversary

In 1988, Lamborghini celebrated its 25th anniversary by introducing a new version of the Countach at the Italian Grand Prix on the Monza circuit.

Mechanically the Countach 25th Anniversary model was similar to the LP 5000 Quattrovalvole. The body sprouted all manner of new air inlets and outlets, which made the car look even wider and more massive than ever. Not everybody liked the facelift but the car was introduced just at the right time.

By the end of 1988, prices for exotic cars such as Ferrari and others had reached unbelievable limits and many speculators ordered the anniversary car hoping that its value would rise fast and high. As a result of this speculation fever no less than 657 examples of the 25th Anniversary car were fabricated, the highest production run, so far for a Countach.

More 25th Anniversary models were built than any other model of the Countach. The subtle redesign of the bodywork brought the car into the 1990s.

Model .Countach 25th Anniversary	Frame . . . . .Tubular
Introduced . . . . .1988 Italian Grand Prix at Monza	**General**
Production years 1988-1990	Wheelbase mm/in. 2500/97.5
Number built 657	Track, front mm/in. 1536/59.9
Engine . . . . .V-12 60°	rear mm/in. 1606/62.6
Bore × stroke in mm .85.5 × 75	Brakes . . . . .Ventilated discs
Displacement in cc 5167	Tire size, front and rear . . . . .225/50 VR and
Valve operation . . . . .Double overhead cam-	345/35 VR 15
shafts on each bank of cylinders. Four	Wheels . . . . .Magnesium; front 8.5, rear 12
valves per cylinder.	Body builder . . . . .Lamborghini
Compression ratio 9.5:1	Fuel tank capacity . . . . .2 × 60 lit
Carburetion . . . . .6 twin-throat Webers, 44 DCNF	Engine oil capacity . . . . .17 lit/18 qt
Bhp . . . . .455 at 7000	Cooling system capacity . . . . .17 lit/18 qt
Chassis & Drivetrain	Overall length mm/in. 4140/161.5
Clutch . . . . .Single dry-plate, hydraulically	Overall width mm/in. .2000/78
operated	Overall height mm/in. 1070/41.7
Transmission . . . . .Five-speed, all-synchromesh	Dry weight kg/lb 1490/3278
Rear suspension . . . . .Independent, coil springs	Top speed km/h/mph 295/183
and telescopic shock absorbers	
Axle ratio 11/45	
Front suspension . . . . .Independent, coil springs	
and telescopic shock absorbers	

The lines of the 25th Anniversary Countach were rather cluttered. The numerous air vents featured the "cookie-cutter" design used early on by Marcello Gandini's Miura and more recently by Ferrari's Testarossa.

Mechanically, the 25th Anniversary Countach was similar to the predecessor Countach LP 5000 Quattrovalvole with the engine producing 455 bhp.

CHAPTER 12
BRAVO

Bertone's stylist Marcello Gandini designed the Bravo. The car, named after a strain of Spanish fighting bulls, was just an exercise or show car, and as the financial situation at Lamborghini was very bad, nobody even hoped they would buy the project. The car was presented at the 1974 Turin motor show and was one of the cleanest designs present. Built on a Urraco chassis, shortened by 20 cm (7.8 in.), it looked a bit like a scaled down Countach. The prototype really ran, Bertone claiming a top speed of 272 km/h (168.6 mph), but it ended up in Bertone's museum.

The Bravo has not been forgotten and Lamborghini's management assured me that the car would be on the production line at the end of 1983. By the time you read this book you will know if this was just wishful thinking.

Bertone used the platform of a Urraco to build this dream car, the Bravo, or as it was called by the factory, Studio 114. The car was shown at the 1974 Turin show and it is clear that not only the wheels were taken for the later Silhouette design. The Bravo prototype is in the Bertone museum now, but early 1983 rumors were that the car might go into production that year.

CHAPTER 13
SILHOUETTE

★★★★

Lamborghini had never made a convertible until the Silhouette. This handsome little car, first shown at the 1976 Geneva show, was built on a strengthened Urraco chassis, keeping the same wheelbase. The monocoque-type body was designed and built by Bertone again and looked very sporty—it was very wide and low.

From the rear the car looked like a racing car with its low-profile tires on eleven-inch wheels. The car had an impressive spoiler on the front, as the fashion of the day dictated, but the Silhouette not only looked sporty, it handled like a sports car. From a standing start it would cover a kilometer in the same time as the Miura SV (twenty-five seconds). And its cornering, very good on the Urraco, was even better now with the wide tires.

The interior of the new car was redesigned and the instruments grouped together in a more practical way with the different switches all on the right-hand side of the panel.

Only fifty-two cars were built of this very desirable model.

Model . . . . **Silhouette**	Frame . . . . Integral chassis/body
Introduced . . . . 1976 Geneva motor show	**General**
Number built . . . . 52 (no. 40.000-40.104)	Wheelbase mm/in. 2450/95.5
Production years 1976-78	Track, front mm/in. 1490/58
Engine . . . . V-8 90° transverse, mid engine	rear mm/in. 1550/60.5
Bore × stroke in mm . . . . 86 × 64.5	Brakes . . . . Girling ventilated discs
Displacement in cc 2995.8	Tire size, front and rear . . . . 195/50 VR 15 and
Valve operation . . . . Single overhead camshafts	285/40 VR 15
on each bank of cylinders	Wheels . . . . Campagnolo cast magnesium 8" and 11"
Compression ratio 10:1	Body builder . . . . Bertone
Carburetion . . . . 4 twin-throat Webers, 40 DCNF	Fuel tank capacity . . . . 80 lit/21 gal
Bhp . . . . 265 at 7800 rpm	Engine oil capacity . . . . 7.5 lit/7.9 qt
Chassis & Drivetrain	Cooling system capacity . . . . 15 lit/15.8 qt
Clutch . . . . . . Single dry-plate, hydraulically operated	Overall length mm/in. 4320/168.5
Transmission . . . . Five-speed, all-synchromesh	Overall width mm/in. 1880/73.3
Rear suspension . . . . Independent, coil springs	Overall height mm/in. 1120/43.7
and telescopic shock absorbers	Dry weight kg/lb. 1240/2728
Axle ratio 14/35	Top speed kmph/mph 260/161.2
Front suspension . . . . . Independent, coil springs and	
telescopic shock absorbers	

Bertone designed and built the Silhouette, with the wheel designed for the Bravo show car. The car certainly looked exciting from the rear, too.

The Silhouette's instrument layout was much better than on the
Urraco coupes.

Some photographs taken before the opening of the 1977 Geneva
motor show. Behind the Silhouette (top) is the Cheetah, which
was the big surprise at the Lamborghini stand.

CHAPTER 14
ATHON

★★★★★

When the Lamborghini factory had its deepest troubles and hopes for recovery had almost been given up, Bertone came to the 1980 Turin show with a Lamborghini Urraco Spider, the Athon. The car, built on the Silhouette chassis, was a support to the dying factory. The Bertone press report read: "At such a testing moment, it is Bertone's intention to once again lend its support to a name [Lamborghini] that it does not want to die."

Though the car was fully drivable it was never intended to become a production car.

The one-off Silhouette, the Athon, did not have a top and was strictly built as a dream car.

Many technical ideas were built into the Athon. The interior shows the steering wheel integrated in the dashboard. The gearshift lever looks a bit clumsy.

CHAPTER 15

JALPA P 350

★★★

When the Mimran family bought the Lamborghini factory in 1981 the decision was made to concentrate on two sports cars only, in addition to the LM 001 jeep. The Countach would remain in production, as would a more modern version of the Silhouette, the Jalpa P 350, introduced at the 1981 Geneva motor show. Of course it was Bertone again who designed the body of this pretty Targa Spider.

Mechanically the layout was the same as on the Silhouette, though the engine now had a capacity of 3.5 liters and an output of 255 hp at 7000 rpm.

Production did not start until the end of 1982, after various prototypes were tested. This small Lamborghini was never a hit and did not sell well even though it was a joy to drive. The targa top could be removed and the quality of the car was superior to that of its predecessors in many ways. By enlarging the stroke of the Urraco P 300 engine, Giulio Alfieri had not only enlarged the volume of the engine from 3 to 3.5 liters, but had also increased the torque from 270 to 310 lb-ft at 3500 rpm enabling the car to accelerate from 30 mph in fifth gear without difficulties.

Model ....**Jalpa P 350**	Frame ....Integral chassis/body
Introduced ....1981 Geneva motor show	**General**
Production years ....1982-1988; 410 cars built	Wheelbase mm/in. 2450/95.5
Engine ....V-8 90° transverse mid engine	Track, front mm/in. 1500/58.5
Bore × stroke in mm ....86 × 75	rear mm/in. 1554/60.6
Displacement in cc 3485	Brakes ....Ventilated discs
Valve operation ....Single overhead camshafts	Tire size, front and rear	205/55 VR 16 and
on each bank of cylinders		225/50 VR 16
Compression ratio 9.2:1	Wheels ....Campagnolo cast magnesium
Carburetion ....4 twin-throat Webers, 42 DCNF	Body builder ....Bertone
Bhp ....255 at 7000 rpm	Fuel tank capacity ....80 lit/21 gal
Chassis & Drivetrain	Engine oil capacity ....9 lit/9.45 qt
Clutch ....Single dry-plate, hydraulically operated	Cooling system capacity ....15 lit/15.8 qt
Transmission ....Five-speed, all-synchromesh	Overall length mm/in. 4330/168.9
Rear suspension ....Independent, coil springs	Overall width mm/in. 1880/73.3
and telescopic shock absorbers	Overall height mm/in. 1140/44.5
Axle ratio 17/68	Dry weight kg/lb 1510/3322
Front suspension ....Independent, coil springs	Top speed kmph/mph 250/155
and telescopic shock absorbers	

For the first time in its history Lamborghini only had a small stand at the 1981 Geneva motor show, but it was big enough to show Bertone's new Targa Spider, the Jalpa P 350.

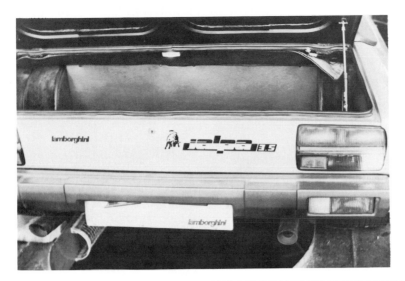

Photographs taken at the factory in May 1982 of a Jalpa back from test runs.

The clean interior of the Jalpa prototype.

CHAPTER 16

CHEETAH

Off-road vehicles were the big hit in the late seventies and every re-spectable European had, or at least dreamed of having, a Blazer, a Jeep or a Rangerover. The big surprise of the 1977 Geneva motor show was that even Lamborghini had jumped into this market.

The Cheetah was built "to open up new horizons for the future of the factory," as a factory press release stated. Lamborghini hoped to sell the car to the American army. The car had a Chrysler V-8 engine, located in a central-rear position, four-wheel drive with two Triple D torque-biasing interaxle differentials and a three-speed Chrysler auto-matic gearbox.

With a full (133-liter, 35-gal) fuel tank the weight of the car was 2,042 kg (4,492 lb.), but it had a claimed top speed of 167 km/h, (103.5 mph), accelerating from 0 to 100 km/h (0-62 mph) in nine seconds.

Like a good Lamborghini it had some options, too. The fiber-reinforced plastic body was fully removable and replaceable by an ar-mored one. The car stood on oversize desert racing tires with safety inner liners, claimed by the factory to be bullet-proof. Other features included special equipment for desert use. The Cheetah was tested by the American army in California, but was totaled there in a crash. The remains stayed in the US, but have not been heard of since.

Model	.... Cheetah
Introduced	.... 1977 Geneva motor show
Number built	1
Production years	1977
Engine	.... Chrysler V-8
Displacement in cc	5900
Bhp	.... 183 at 4000 rpm

Chassis & Drivetrain

Transmission	.... Chrysler A 727 automatic
Rear suspension	..... Independent, torsion bars and telescopic shock absorbers
Axle ratio	.... 3.27/1 to 5.89/1
Rear suspension	..... Independent, torsion bars and
Front suspension	..... Independent, torsion bars and telescopic shock absorbers
Frame	.... Tubular

General

Wheelbase mm/in	........................3000/117
Track, front mm/in	....................1520/59.3
rear mm/in	....................1520/59.3
Brakes	.... Ventilated disc brakes (Countach)
Tire size, front and rear	.... 35.6 x 98.6
Wheels	.... Steel
Body builder	.... Lamborghini
Fuel tank capacity	.... 133 lit/34.9 gal
Engine oil capacity	.... 7.6 lit/8 qt
Cooling system capacity	.... 17 lit/17.9 qt
Overall length mm/in	.... 4320/168.5
Overall width mm/in	.... 1880/73.3
Overall height mm/in	.... 1580/61.6
Dry weight kg/lb	.................2042/4492
Top speed kmph/mph	.... 167/103.5

The Cheetah at the 1977 Geneva motor show. At least the interior looked like a Lamborghini.

Nuova Automobili Ferruccio Lamborghini SpA could not forget the off-road project and returned to Geneva with a similar car in 1981. This time the car was named LM 001 and it was driven by a 5.9-liter AMC engine coupled to a Chrysler automatic transmission. The car was capable of a top speed of 150 km/h (93 mph) on roads, or 120 km/h (74.4 mph) in the desert. Giving up the hope to sell the car to the American army, after the bad presentation of the Cheetah, promotions were aimed toward the desert countries and brochures were handed out in Arabic languages. The car did not go into production; but, still, the project remained under consideration.

LM 002

To make the LM 001 a truly exceptional car the AMC engine was replaced by a 4754 cc V-12 Lamborghini unit with an output of 332 hp at 6000 rpm. No more automatic transmission, but a five-speed manual ZF box instead. And, of course, four-wheel drive.

The LM 002 performed like a racing car and, though the weight was 2,600 kg (5,720 lb.), with a full 280-liter (73.5 gal) fuel tank, the top speed was 188 km/h (116.6 mph), reaching 100 km/h (62 mph) on the speedometer from zero in twelve seconds.

The factory thought a market could be found in the Arabic countries; so the car was taken to the desert for extensive tests. There the problems started. The engine got too hot, the brakes were insufficient and, worse yet, while driving at high speeds across the dunes, the front end of the car lifted up in the air. Ing. Alfieri knew only one solution: Put the engine in the front of the car—and that is how the LMA was born.

LMA

The LMA (Lamborghini Military Anteriore = front) is nothing but the LM 002 with the Lamborghini V-12 engine mounted in the front, mated with a Countach five-speed gearbox. Bringing the engine to the front of the car brought advantages as well. The weight ratio became fifty-fifty and extra room for luggage or passengers was created behind the front seats.

The car was built on a tube chassis strengthened by steel plating. The torsion bar suspension, used on the Cheetah, was replaced by coil springs. The top speed of 188 km/h (116.6 mph) and the acceleration of the LMA were the same as for the LM 002, but the roadholding at high speeds was much better now.

In the desert the car behaved as Alfieri had expected, though the ground clearance of 295 mm (11.5 in.) under the differentials might

At the 1981 Geneva motor show Ing. Alfieri is smiling behind the car.

The LM 001.

be rather low. Still, several armies have contacted the factory concerning the car. The car became available to the general public in 1986 under the name LM 002, for a price one had to pay for a Countach. It was meant to sell as the LMA, (for Lamborghini-Mimran-Anteriore, named after the owner of the factory, Patrick Mimran, who did so much for the project), but then this idea was changed.

Model	**LM 001**
Introduced	1981 Geneva motor show
Number built	1
Production years	1981
Engine	AMC V-8
Displacement in cc	5900
Bhp	180 at 4000 rpm
Chassis & Drivetrain	
Transmission	Chrysler A 727 automatic
Rear suspension	Independent, torsion bars and telescopic shock absorbers
Front suspension	Independent, torsion bars and telescopic shock absorbers
Frame	Tubular
General	
Wheelbase mm/in.	2950/115
Track, front mm/in.	1615/63
rear mm/in.	1615/63
Brakes	Ventilated disc brakes (Countach)
Tire size, front and rear	14 x 16 LT
Wheels	Steel
Body builder	Lamborghini
Fuel tank capacity	190 lit/50 gal
Engine oil capacity	7.6 lit/8 qt
Cooling system capacity	17 lit/17.9 qt
Overall length mm/in.	4790/186.8
Overall width mm/in.	2000/78
Overall height mm/in.	1790/69.8
Dry weight kg/lb.	2100/4620
Top speed kmph/mph	160/99.2

Model	**LMA**
Introduced	1982 Geneva motor show
Number built	1
Production years	1982 to date
Engine	V-12 60° L.503
Displacement in cc	4754 or 7 liters or diesel
Valve operation	Double overhead camshafts on each bank of cylinders
Bhp	332 at 6000 rpm
Chassis & Drivetrain	
Clutch	Single dry-plate, hydraulically operated
Transmission	Five-speed, all-synchromesh
Rear suspension	Independent, coil springs and telescopic shock absorbers
Front suspension	Independent, coil springs and telescopic shock absorbers
Frame	Tubular
General	
Wheelbase mm/in.	2950/115
Track, front mm/in.	1615/63
rear mm/in.	1615/63
Brakes	Ventilated disc (Countach)
Tire size, front and rear	14 x 16 LT
Wheels	Steel 16" x 9"
Body builder	Lamborghini
Fuel tank capacity	280 lit/73.5 gal
Engine oil capacity	17.5 lit/18.4 qt
Cooling system capacity	17 lit/17.9 qt
Overall length mm/in.	4790/186.8
Overall width mm/in.	2000/78
Overall height mm/in.	1850/72
Dry weight kg/lb.	2600/5720
Top speed kmph/mph	188/116.6

Model	**LM 002**
Introduced	1982 Geneva motor show
Number built	still in production
Production years	1986-
Engine	V-12 60° L.510
Displacement in cc	5167
Valve operation	Double overhead camshafts on each bank of cylinders. Four valves per cylinder.
Bhp	450 at 6800 rpm
Chassis & Drivetrain	
Clutch	Single dry-plate, hydraulically operated
Transmission	Five-speed, all synchromesh. Z.F. S5-24/3
Rear suspension	Independent, coil springs and telescopic shock absorbers
Front suspension	Independent, coil springs and telescopic shock absorbers
Frame	Tubular
General	
Wheelbase mm/in.	3000/117
Track, front mm/in.	1615/62.9
rear mm/in.	1615/62.9
Brakes	Front: Ventilated discs. Rear: Drums 12×3
Tire size, front and rear	325/65 VR 17
Wheels	Steel 17×11
Body builder	Lamborghini
Fuel tank capacity	290 lit 76 qt
Fuel tank capacity	290 lit 76 qt
Engine oil capacity	17.5 lit/18.4 qt
Cooling system capacity	17 lit/17.8 qt
Overall length mm/in.	4900/191
Overall width mm/in.	2000/78
Overall height mm/in.	1850/72
Dry weight kg/lb.	2700/5940
Top speed kmph/mph	201/124.6

The LMA, that should become the LM 002 once production starts, was first shown to the public a few minutes before the Monaco Grand Prix started in 1982. These photographs were taken at the factory the day after the race.

The LM 002 can drive with a speed of over 200 km/h and will accelerate from 0 to 100 km/h in 8.5 seconds.

Next to five comfortable seats in the car, there is space for six more outside.

The four-valve Countach engine has an output of no less than 450
hp at 6800 rpm.

On the 1987 Geneva motor show Lamborghini showed the LM 002
as a rolling chassis.

LM 004/7000

At the 1985 Geneva motor show another prototype of the off-road car was shown. This time a 7257 cc V-12 powerboat engine was coupled with a five-speed ZF gearbox. With a top speed of 206 km/h (128 mph) it was almost certainly the fastest off-road car in the world, but who needed it? The car could accelerate from 0 to 100 km/h in 8.5 seconds and climb a 125 percent grade in first gear.

Model . . . .**LM 004/7000**	Frame . . . . .Tubular
Introduced . . . . .1985 Geneva motor show	**General**
Production years . . . . .1985, 1 prototype built	Wheelbase mm/in. 3000/117
Engine . . . . .V-12 off-shore boat engine	Track, front mm/in. 1615/63
Displacement in cc .7257	rear mm/in. 1615/63
Valve operation . . . . .Double overhead camshafts	Brakes . . . . .Ventilated discs
on each bank of cylinders	Tire size, front and rear . . . . .325/65 VR 17
Bhp 420	Wheels . . . . .Steel, 17 × 11″
Chassis & Drivetrain	Body builder . . . . .Lamborghini
Clutch . . . . .Single dry-plate, hydraulically operated	Fuel tank capacity . . . . .320 lit/84 gal
Transmission . . . . .Five-speed, all-synchromesh	Engine oil capacity . . . . .17.5 lit/18.4 qt
Rear suspension . . . . .Independent, coil springs	Cooling system capacity . . . . .17 lit/17.8 qt
and telescopic shock absorbers	Overall length mm/in. 4900/191
Front suspension . . . . .Independent, coil springs	Overall width mm/in. 2000/78
and telescopic shock absorbers	Overall height mm/in. 1850/72
	Dry weight kg/lb .2700/5940
	Top speed km/h/mph 206/128

The LM-004/7000 was based around Lamborghini's 7.3 liter powerboat engine. Even with the hefty off-road drivetrain and the tall tires, the LM 004 could reach a top speed of 206 km/h or 128 mph.

Side view of the LM 004/7000.

CHAPTER 18
PORTOFINO

At the Frankfurt motor show in the autumn of 1987, Chrysler presented a concept car, called the Portofino. This car was created by Chrysler Motors' international design team and the body was built by Coggiola of Turin, Italy. Lamborghini had been responsible for the mechanics and a 3485 cc V-8 Jalpa engine was located in front of the rear axle. The doors, like those on the Countach, pivoted up and out of the way to allow for ease of entry. The running prototype reached a top speed of 240 km/h (149 mph) as a result of its advanced aerodynamic styling.

The Portofino was a concept car built by Chrysler, and was first shown at the 1987 Frankfurt motor show. The car was based on the mechanics of the Jalpa, using the 3.5 liter V-8 engine.

At the 1988 Turin motor show, Bertone presented another dream car built with the mechanics of a Lamborghini. Some 30,000 man hours had been invested in the Genesis, a futuristic family car. A shortened chassis with the 265 cm wheelbase of a Lamborghini Espada was used for this five seater. As with the original Espada, the V-12 engine was mounted in the front of the chassis but this time the five-speed gearbox was replaced by a Torqueflite automatic gearbox from the Chrysler factory.

In the summer of 1991 there were rumors that the Lamborghini LM 002 was to be phased out of production (238 having been built between 1986 and the end of 1990) so why not replace the "Jeep" by a more suitable car like the Genesis?

The five-seater Bertone-Lamborghini Genesis was first shown on the carrozzeria's stand at the 1988 Turin motor show.

CHAPTER 20

DIABLO

In January 1990, nineteen years after the Countach was first shown, Lamborghini introduced its successor, the Diablo, or Devil, in Monaco. In November 1985, Marcello Gandini had started work on the design of the car and six months later, one year before Chrysler came into the picture, a full-scale model was ready. Development work began seriously when the Chrysler dollars became available and soon a second prototype was built at the Chrysler studios in Detroit.

The Diablo stood on a longer wheelbase than the Countach and was 200 kg (442 lb.) heavier due to the many electric motors that operated the seats and door windows and the fact that the chassis was laid out for a four-wheel-drive version due to appear late in 1991. The overall length was only 2 cm (0.78 in.) longer due to the short nose and rear overhang of the Diablo. The track was also changed with a reduction of 2 cm (0.78 in.) at the front and an increase of 4 cm (1.56 in.) at the rear.

Early cars were shod with Pirelli P Zero tires but soon all Diablos were fitted with Bridgestone RE 71 tires. No spare tire was to be found in the car.

Like the Countach, the Diablo was built on a tubular frame but this time tubes with a square profile were chosen. Most of the body was made of aluminum alloy but the floor panels, the trunk and engine lid were made of carbon fiber.

The Diablo had doors similar to those used on the Countach and just as many air inlets and outlets. The inlets in front of the rear wheels led the air to the oil cooler and air conditioning; those behind the side windows carried air to the water radiators, which were situated in the rear of the car.

The Diablo reached a top speed of 323 km/h (200 mph) in fifth gear with the engine producing 492 bhp at 7000 rpm. In July 1987, Ferrari introduced its new supercar, the F40, but here the twin-turbo V-8 produced "only" 478 bhp.

The Diablo was not an easy car to drive as in town, when driving at slow speeds, the steering was heavy and the clutch and brake pedal needed strong legs. But unlike the Countach, the Diablo was easier to park when reversing as the rear window was bigger and useful rather than cosmetic. The instrument panel was in the field of vision and adjustable for height so that it could be lowered in towns and raised when the car was driven fast on the highways.

Model ....**Diablo**	Frame ....Tubular
Introduced ....January 1990 at Monaco	**General**
Production years 1990-today	Wheelbase mm/in 2650/103.3
Engine ....V-12 60°	Track, front mm/in 1540/60
Bore x stroke in mm ....87 x 80	rear mm/in 1640/64
Displacement in cc 5703	Brakes ....Ventilated discs
Valve operation ....Double overhead camshafts	Tire size, front and rear .....245/40 ZR 17 and 335/35 ZR 17
on each bank of cylinders	Wheels ....Magnesium; front 8.5 J, rear 13 J
Compression ratio 10.0:1	Body builder ....Lamborghini after design by Gandini
Carburetion ....Weber fuel injection	Fuel tank capacity ....100 lit/106 qt
Bhp ....492 at 7000 rpm	Engine oil capacity ....13 lit/14 qt
Chassis & Drivetrain	Overall length mm/in 4460/174
Clutch ....Single dry-plate, hydraulically operated	Overall width mm/in 2040/79.5
Transmission ....Five-speed, all-synchromesh	Overall height mm/in 1100/43
Rear suspension ....Independent, coil springs	Dry weight kg/lb 1650/1815
and telescopic shock absorbers	Top speed km/h/mph 325/201.5
Axle ratio 3.83:1	
Front suspension ....Independent, coil springs	
and telescopic shock absorbers	

The Diablo was designed by Marcello Gandini, the man who penned the lines of the Miura and Countach.

For the United States, the Diablo engine with catalytic converter had an output of 86.3 bhp per liter of displacement—a total of 492 bhp at 7000 rpm.

The design of the Diablo smoothed over many of the excesses of the Countach's bodywork and resulted in more streamlined, modern styling.

The Diablo retained the upward-swinging, front-pivoting doors of the Countach but ingress was made much easier. The rear window was also usable on the Diablo whereas it had been largely ornamental on the Countach.

At the end of July 1988, the Jalpa was taken out of production. With only 410 cars built in six years the model had been no great success. Ing. Marmiroli had by then started working on a new family of Vee engines that could be built with six, eight, ten or twelve cylinders. Of course all engines carried four overhead camshafts, breathed through four valves per cylinder and got their fuel-air mixture through an electronic fuel-injection system.

In November 1988, Lamborghini dealers visiting the factory were shown a model of the successor of the Jalpa, known as the P 140, and even if this was not the final shape it can be said that the new car will have a targa top and probably be powered by a V-10 engine.

Different styling models had been made. One came from Lamborghini's styling department, two were made in the United States by Chrysler, Marcello Gandini made one and of course Bertone was also given the opportunity. The car shown was a mixture of the Bertone car and one of the Chrysler proposals. Will the real car look like it? We will know in 1993 when the P 140 is finally released.

Early design rendering for the mid-engined V-10 P 140. Is this what the successor of the Jalpa will look like?

CLUBS AND SOURCES

The following addresses might be of help to you:

Classic Motorbooks
P.O. Box 1
Osceola, WI 54020 USA

Bob Wallace Cars, Inc.
2310 E. Magnolia St.
Phoenix, AZ 85034 USA

Nuova Automobili Ferruccio Lamborghini SpA
40019 S. Agata Bolognese (Bologna) Italy
Tel (051) 956171, Telex 510278 LAMBOR I

Lamborghini of North America
25524 Frampton Avenue, Harbor City, CA 90710
Tel (213) 325-1271

International Lamborghini Owners Club E.V.
Köllns Acker 5, 2000 Hamburg 54, Germany
Tel (040) 577571

and its representatives:

Australia: A. A. de Fina, 28 Linacre Rd.
                Hampton, Victoria

Canada: Ken Browning, P.O. Box 543,
                Tillsonburg, Ontario

France: Ciclet Avenue de Garlande 7,
                92220 Bagneux

Luxembourg: John Wengler, Rosport, Rue
                du Barrage

Austria: Manfred Dobisch, 3. Ober-
                zellergasse 18/18 1140 Wien

Saudi Arabia: Michel James Bonney, c/o Brit-
                ish Aircraft Corp. P.O. Box 1732,
                Riyadh

Sweden: Leif Nilsson, Blabärsgatan
                8.23400, Lomma

Switzerland: Dr. Urs Blum, Kirchgasse 33,
                8001 Zürich

Great Britain: Peter Dew, 30 Ruston Mews,
                London W 2
                Mike Pullen, 44 Sussex Road,
                Haywards Heath, Sussex

Lamborghini Club America
Jim Heady
170 Monte Vista Road
Orinda, CA 94563

INDEX